BUT YOU DON'T UNDERSTAND!

By *Elaine Sishton* and *Charlotte Russell*
Illustrated by *Richard Duszczak*

•

LIFE: THIS WAY Series
Created by *Lesley Pollinger*

John HUNT Publishing

Copyright © 2000 John Hunt Publishing Ltd.

Text © 2000 Elaine Sishton and Charlotte Russell

Illustrations © 2000 Richard Duszczak

ISBN 1 903019 66 4

Designed by
ANDREW MILNE DESIGN

All rights reserved. Except for brief quotations in critical articles or reviews, no part of this book may be reproduced in any manner without prior written permission from the publishers.

Write to John Hunt Publishing Ltd
46a West Street, Alresford, Hampshire SO24 9AU, UK

The rights of Elaine Sishton and Charlotte Russell as authors and Richard Duszczak illustrator of this work have been asserted in accordance with the Copyright, Designs and Patents Act 1988.

A CIP catalogue record for this book is available from the British Library.

Printed in Singapore

With thanks to

Christine Evans, Head of Lifeskills Department,
France Hill School, Frimley, Surrey

Iain Brown, Katy and Dave Loffman for their
support and editorial input.

The students of Great Wyrley High School, Staffordshire
for invaluable quotes and comments.

Crystal and Bethany Hadcroft, John Hunt and Andrew Milne
for their courage and patience.

LIFE: THIS WAY series and characters created by Lesley Pollinger

CONTENTS

CHAPTER 1
BUT YOU DON'T UNDERSTAND 5
Feeling misunderstood is a common experience in adolescence

CHAPTER 2
RULES, RULES, JUST FOR FOOLS 17
Gangs and rebels, crime and punishment

CHAPTER 3
FRUSTRATION! 31
Frustration, anger, rage and unacceptable situations

CHAPTER 4
JUST A PHYSICAL ATTRACTION? 47
Good friends, making friends and friendship changes

CHAPTER 5
DO YA LOVE ME? 61
Different kinds of love, sex and decisions

CHAPTER 6
DUMPSVILLE! 81
How to cope with being rejected by someone and how to end a relationship

CHAPTER 7
THE SAME BUT DIFFERENT 99
Trends and fashions, physical and mental differences including homosexuality and disability

CHAPTER 8
US AND THEM 111
Discussing prejudice, attitudes and discrimination

CHAPTER 9
IT'S A GOAL! 123
Needs and wants, hopes and ambitions and goals

CHAPTER 10
SLUGS AND SPICE 133
Different male and female viewpoints

APPENDIX
USEFUL CONTACTS (UK) 138

 LIFE: THIS WAY

Chapter 1
BUT YOU DON'T UNDERSTAND!

They'd understand each other better if they listened to what was being said!

Being understood

This is a book about something very important to everyone: being understood.

Have you ever told someone something which is really important to you, only to realise that they haven't understood a word of what you've been trying to say, or worse, haven't even been listening? It may be that the person you were talking to is concentrating on something else at the time or has other things on their mind.

If you look carefully at the 'listener's' body language, you may be able to read the signs.

Is the person you are trying to communicate with engaging in eye contact and looking directly at you? Are they nodding as if they are understanding and listening when you speak? Are they asking questions back, or mmming in agreement, or making comments? Are they facing away from you, or watching the television / on level 216 of a computer game / reading the paper / on the 'phone / working on plans for a new aerodynamic lawnmower with interactive communication? Have you actually picked a good moment to say what you want to be heard?

Adolescence

You may experience really difficult times from a relationship point of view, both with family and friends during the adolescent years, say between the ages of 11 and 16. It's a period when so many physical, psychological and emotional changes are taking place that it's only natural for you to feel alone, afraid and sometimes misunderstood.

You are becoming more independent as you prepare for adulthood and may resent any adult interference in things you believe you can work out for yourself. Every little detail of daily life could potentially lead to conflict and arguments with your family and others.

> *When I fall out with my parents, especially my dad, it's about little things to begin with, but then it escalates and I find other things which irritate me about them. We are both too stubborn to say sorry to each other so it lasts for days. I can never fall out with my mum for long though, and we always make up.*
>
> (17-YEAR-OLD GIRL)

As a teenager you fall between the stages of 'child' and 'adult' (no wonder it's confusing – you're neither one thing nor the other). Adults treat you like a child one minute and you feel they are not recognising how mature you are, then the next moment you might be given so many things to do and remember you don't know how to cope! There may be days when you think you can take on the world and you have a solution for everything, and others where

you desperately want someone else to take control of a situation. Taking responsibility without being asked, though, is certainly one way of showing others just how mature you are becoming.

Emotions

Your emotions are all over the place too, because of all of the physical, hormonal and mentally maturing changes you are experiencing and you will naturally feel some things very intensely. Mood swings (perhaps triggered by a really quite trivial event) may range from blissful happiness to the depths of despair, and contribute to this feeling that no-one understands. These can happen very quickly and it's difficult for both you and your family to understand when something tiny and unimportant can produce an absolute explosion of emotions.

BUT YOU DON'T UNDERSTAND

When you are wrapped up in your own feelings, you may also fail to see the effect your moods, irritability and quick temper have on others. You probably also take your family for granted, which doesn't lead the way to good relationships. Very often there's a breakdown in communication so that you don't understand adults and they seem not to understand you.

> *I argue with my parents, but especially my mum because she treats me like a child when I want to be independent. She tries to control a lot of things that I do and I want more privacy than she lets me have!*
>
> (16-YEAR-OLD GIRL)

When you're feeling hard done-by and misunderstood, your parents and family may start to find you unpleasant and difficult to live with. It's a big shock to find that their lovely little child with the enormous smile who was so dependent and loving suddenly asserts themselves and demands their independence. They find it hard to understand what has happened to their little Miss or Master Sunshine who was always happy and enjoyed life and never caused any real trouble.

> *Lately I argue with my parents about virtually anything. They think I go out too much, don't do enough schoolwork, spend too much money, don't save enough money, don't help enough around the house and anything else they can blame me for. I just smile and walk away because I know it's not worth arguing about. I then go out with my best friend who always cheers me up.*
>
> (17-YEAR-OLD GIRL)

Friends

Your natural demand for independence means you may make a conscious shift away from your family towards your friends, and this could make your parents feel unwanted and rejected. You no longer seem happy to be always in the company of your family and doing family things together and sometimes you make this resentment perfectly clear!

You reach a stage where relationships with your friends often become the most important ones in your life. You may not be willing to talk about your feelings to any of the adults in your family, but prefer your friends. You may want to be with them every available minute and resent anyone else trying to 'butt in'. Friends of your own age know what you're going through and how you're feeling, because they're going through exactly the same thing.

More than friends

You also begin to notice and be attracted to the opposite sex and even fall in love for the first time. Your first experience of love may

be with someone of the same sex or someone you admire – like a teacher or movie star (but more about this later). Love relationships in themselves may also cause problems at home. Perhaps your family isn't too keen on some of your friends, or you aren't allowed to spend as much time as you'd like with your boy or girlfriend.

Your resentment builds up towards the thousands of rules that you suddenly have to stick to and the adults who try and enforce them, at times as if to spite you. Some of you may kick against these rules and go too far, with devastating results, as we look at in the next chapter.

'Sharing a room with my brother can sometimes cause rows. One row that usually occurs is about what goes on TV, or what to listen to whilst doing homework. In one case this has led to my brother breaking a chair and kicking a hole in the door.'

'Sharing a bedroom with my brother is sometimes annoying. As he is older we mostly have to watch what he wants and listen to what he wants to, and he snores which keeps me awake at night.'

(TWIN 17-YEAR-OLD BROTHERS)

This book also looks at some of the darker sides of human nature, such as crime, aggression and frustration; it suggests ways to control them and how to deal with them in life. Rejection, prejudice and differences between people are considered, as these are important issues which need understanding.

Dealing with issues and developing your 'self'

What all the issues in the following chapters do, and what they all have in common, is to help you to grow as a person. They help to mould you into the adult you are becoming. Your 'self' develops and along with that you begin to set goals for your future. The development of an awareness of 'self' is an important part of adolescence. It brings with it the power to compare and contrast relationships as well as making assessments and judgements about important matters.

You become interested in yourself as a person and see the world through new eyes. A new attitude of mind emerges which can throw you a bit at first. Your family relationships alter and so do those with your friends. All of these changes can make you feel very unsure of everything that you've previously been sure of.

Criticism

When feeling so uncertain it's not surprising that most of us become very sensitive to criticism from others. You may be accused of:

- arguing
- moodiness
- laziness
- rudeness
- grumbling
- being untidy
- jealousy
- being selfish
- thoughtlessness
- irresponsibility
- being unreasonable
- dissatisfaction
- lack of interest in appearance
- too much interest in appearance
- upsetting the family
- lacking concentration
- being noisy
- not doing your homework
- being unkind

No wonder you sometimes feel lost and as though no-one understands you. You may think too that the criticisms are unfair, but deep down know that there may be a grain of truth in some of them. Along with feeling misunderstood you can also feel that you can do absolutely nothing right and be so discouraged that you decide not to make any effort at all. This is a vicious circle because it only brings more moans and criticisms from those around you.

LIFE: THIS WAY

'Being an only child when anything goes wrong or missing means it's always my fault. This causes huge rows in our house.'

(16-YEAR-OLD GIRL)

You'll probably want to spend more time alone to think things through. If you have the luxury of your own room, this is all well and good. But to many this is unfortunately not available and can add to your stress, especially if you live in a crowded home with no privacy, trying to keep your things safe from the prying fingers of others.

'When sharing a bedroom with a sibling, many conflicts arise, especially who controls the radio and television. A major problem is that we get up at different times and tend to wake each other up earlier than normal, which is never a good thing.'

(17-YEAR-OLD BOY)

A major part of growing up and older is about learning to be independent. This independence will equip you to leave your family home and learn to survive in the outside world, and for the rest of your life. Hopefully this book will go some way towards helping you to realise why we sometimes behave as we do and how to handle ourselves and those important parts of your life. It may also help you and the adults around you to 'understand' each other a little better.

BUT YOU DON'T UNDERSTAND

Chaz, Shaz and Baz understand that not everyone lives in a family home with two parents, and that everyone's situation is different. So for 'parents' read 'carers'; for 'school' read 'work / college', and so on, whatever is appropriate for you.

LIFE: THIS WAY

Chapter 2

RULES, RULES, JUST FOR FOOLS

There are times when you hate rules. So do all of your friends. Rules at home, rules at school, rules when you're walking along the street. Rules everywhere! Why? Some of them don't seem to have any rhyme or reason to them. But many are there for a purpose, usually to protect you and other people.

 LIFE: THIS WAY

Growing up

Do you remember when you were still a small child? Most 'rules' were for your own safety and protection:

Chances are that you couldn't wait to be treated like an adult – to be allowed to go to the shops on your own, take a bus, choose how to spend your own money. No more rules! But it doesn't work out quite like that, somehow. With adolescence seems to come even more rules and responsibilities. It's probably not at all like you imagined!

The truth is you can't rush growing up: it takes time. If you do charge at it like a bull at a gate, then you may miss out on one of the most exciting times of your life. Part of growing up is about making mistakes and wrong decisions for yourself and learning from them, so that next time you meet a similar challenge you'll know the right way forward.

As well as coping with enormous physical and mental changes there are other pressures and outside factors to deal with. The rules that you're asked to stick to are usually there to help you, not to cause you grief! These rules could range from turning up at the right place on time (like school, work or an appointment) to getting a driving licence and insurance cover.

Rights and wrongs

As you grow you learn very gradually what is considered to be right and wrong in your family and in society. You come to realise that there are rules and laws to be obeyed and that if you break these rules you'll have to answer to someone in a position of authority (like a teacher or employer). If laws are broken then the police and/or government agencies (like social services) may become involved.

You begin to see the world through new eyes as you begin adolescence. Your own values and beliefs develop, based on how you feel and on experiences that you've had in the past.

It's also a time when you may think that your family or society doesn't understand you at all. No-one cares about how you're feeling and they certainly don't seem to care about you.

When you feel like this, and it's true that everyone has felt it at some time, you may tend to turn away from your family and towards your friends. Being accepted by your peer (friendship) group becomes very important to you.

Some people will act irresponsibly such as:

- **staying out all night**
- **playing truant from school**
- **pretending to be ill**
- **telling lies.**

Some of these actions, and many more you can think of, are a kind of cry for help: 'Look at me, I want to be noticed!' Bad behaviour is certainly a way of attracting attention from all sorts of people around you, but the grief and unhappiness it can cause you doesn't usually give you the result you wanted. In fact it can lead to another vicious circle.

Gangs

Being in a gang or part of a group can make you feel you belong. It's good to share similar interests and thoughts and feelings. Sometimes though gangs can attract people who like making trouble or who want to feel powerful. Bully types often like to be seen as leaders in gang situations. It may be the only place where they can feel in control of their lives. This can lead to trouble.

Rivalry often exists within groups of friends and gangs, and this too can lead to jealousy, spite and even violence. While being in a gang can often be fun, sometimes you may be asked to do something you're not happy with. A crowd mentality can build up and you find yourself being convinced that something you would normally never do seems like a good idea. Just remember that you're an individual and needn't go along with others just for the sake of it.

(Although sometimes that may feel the easiest thing to do!) If you're dared to do anything risky or illegal, then the person doing the daring isn't a true friend.

> *'It's difficult to say 'no' to close friends sometimes. Some of my mates thieve things from shops then brag about it. I feel that I don't fit in because I haven't.'*
> (15-YEAR-OLD GIRL)

It's important to be able to know the rights and wrongs of a situation when this happens, especially if you know it's dangerous or against the law. Listen to that little voice of conscience inside you, don't be carried along in a rush without pausing to think. Have the strength to follow your feelings and say 'no' even if it is hard at the time. Only half an hour later you may realise how right you were. You soon realise that as you go through life you'll have many different relationships. Some last, some won't. Your personality though, is shaped by how you respond to others and decisions that you make.

So how do you say 'no'?

- Take a step back from the situation or take time out. This could be by 'suddenly remembering' you need to be somewhere else urgently.

- Take responsibility and use 'I' instead of 'we'.

- Say you don't want to do it firmly but not aggressively.

- Give a reason as to why you don't want to be a part of something, and repeat that same reason.

- Walk away.

- Look the other(s) in the eye clearly when you say no. Keep repeating yourself if other arguments are put forward.

- Remember it takes more courage to say 'no' than to agree.

- Know that you don't have to do it. It's all down to your choice.

Can you think of any other ideas? Understand that you may earn more respect from others by not being a sheep.

Gangs also tend to be frowned upon by adults, which may make them even more attractive to you. A gang can often behave unsociably, hanging around public places at unreasonable times creating noise, litter and destruction, and causing great upset to others. It's worth thinking about what you're getting out of being with a gang. Sometimes the benefits are not worth the hassle.

Rebels

Knowing all of this some people decide to show they're 'grown up' and independent by rebelling against their family (and sometimes their true friends) and society. They may feel angry or unwanted or feel they have no future. Breaking the rules, any rules, is a way of getting back at everyone and everything. Perhaps some people feel this way because of:

- **no money**
- **no job prospects**
- **low self-esteem**
- **being unhappy**
- **poor living conditions**
- **not being understood**
- **not liking themselves**
- **feeling bored or angry**
- **nothing to do for young people**
- **seeing other people commit crime and get away with it**
- **poor family relationships**
- **bad communication skills**

You may know someone who seems to give others and themselves a constantly hard time. If you knew more about their background and situation, you may start to find some explanation as to why they have become like they are now.

Criminal types?

When people turn to crime it's often because they think that they've got nothing to lose. They may think it's exciting, or daring, brave or clever. Of course this isn't true. Turning to any sort of crime means that you will eventually get caught. Then you may have made a bad situation worse, and one which can lead to a vicious downward spiral.

Those who are caught will often try to give reasons for their unsociable behaviour such as:

- **so others will look up to them**
- **dissatisfaction with life**
- **to improve lifestyle**
- **not thinking about the effects of their actions**
- **done on the spur of the moment**
- **upset after a quarrel**
- **belief that they could get away with it**
- **peer pressure**
- **anger**
- **jealousy of others**
- **family arguments**
- **adult pressure**
- **to get attention**
- **testing boundaries**
- **to solve a problem**

So even though it's normal for you to want to express your independence in the way you behave, if you break too many rules and this leads to breaking the law, then this can definitely put you at risk of messing up this part of your life.

Crime

There's a big difference between being in trouble (getting home late) and committing a crime. Stealing from others is theft. Everything is owned by someone, whether it's a purse, a piece of land or a transport system. Someone somewhere has worked hard to get what they have or create something. It's not yours for the taking without payment, whether you dodge a bus fare or pocket an item from a big supermarket. And it's not yours to damage. But sometimes things that you do without thinking can make you cross the line between getting into trouble and breaking the law. Going along with someone who commits a crime, or even egging them on, are crimes in themselves.

> 'I got into trouble with the police one night and was scared to death. A gang of us were just standing near a 'phone box and this woman reported us for vandalising it. the police came and took our names and addresses even though we hadn't done anything wrong.'
> (14-YEAR-OLD GIRL)

If you break the law and get found out, you'll be arrested. Our legal system, although often a very slow process, is as fair as possible – but that doesn't mean that it's a pleasant experience when the police become involved. If you are arrested the best thing to do is to co-operate. What happens after will depend on your age and the offence you're accused of, and your attitude. A person may be given a verbal warning or caution if it is considered that they are unlikely to commit another offence. After this first warning or reprimand, if the person offends again they will receive a final warning, and when next caught it's straight off to court!

Some people – if considered a danger or liable to escape – can be held in custody (in police cells, remand centres, secure accommodation or prison) until they appear in court. Once at court both sides give evidence and the magistrates or judge and jury will consider it. The court will then make a decision on whether someone is found guilty or not guilty, and if guilty, then a punishment will be decided.

Police powers

The police have the power to stop you even if they only suspect you've broken the law. Even if you haven't done anything wrong it's important not to run away or resist arrest. Stay calm and co-operate. Listen carefully to what you are asked and told. Be rational and be sensible. If you don't understand something then ask, but be polite. If you want to be treated fairly, then be fair yourself.

If you're ever convicted of a crime, a record will be made. This can affect your job prospects (you would have to tell your would-be employer, or in some job cases the employer will do a search for any criminal records) and your choice of career.

If ever you've committed a crime or been tempted, think about the effects of your actions on others. It may be that you have already done something wrong and are feeling guilty about it. You need to talk it through with someone you trust. Get help before you find yourself in an even more serious situation. It's never too late to get help and guidance. Turn to someone you can really trust, and ask to speak with them in confidence.

Self-abuse

Turning to substance abuse is another way that some people kick against the rules or feel they can escape from an unhappy situation. No-one ever thinks they'll get hooked on drugs, alcohol or other substances. It's the old 'it'll never happen to me' syndrome. But the truth is, they do. It's also true that alcohol and drugs are more and more becoming factors in crimes. This may be because drugs are expensive. Suppliers will raise their prices as a person depends on them more. This can lead to stealing to get money for drugs. It can even lead to violence or prostitution.

Any substance that you introduce into your body will affect how the body works. Some substances can affect you physically, mentally and emotionally. It's easy to become 'out of control' and do things that you normally wouldn't do. Drugs especially can alter your thinking about what's right and wrong, and what's real and what isn't.

If you know someone close who has a problem with substance abuse, there are many people and organisations who can help. Their own doctor could be the first port of call. But the person has got to want help and want to get clean, otherwise no amount of help will do any good.

Staying clean

Really it's up to you. It's your decision and your responsibility. You and only you, can decide if it's worth it. Taking drugs or getting into trouble with the police could have long-lasting and devastating effects for you in the end.

Stay aware of risk situations and don't do things that you feel unhappy about. Committing a crime, or taking illegal substances may give you a 'high' at first, but when you're caught will you think 'yes, it was worth it?'.

BUT YOU DON'T UNDERSTAND 29

 LIFE: THIS WAY

Chapter 3
FRUSTRATION!

Frustration and aggression

Whenever you're stopped from doing something you really want to do or are blocked from reaching an important goal, you may become frustrated. In turn this can lead to aggressive thoughts or behaviour planned to remove the person or object causing the frustration. If you've been aggressive in the past and have been punished for it, then you may realise it's not acceptable and your frustration needs to find another way out. Breaking something, yelling abuse, swearing, physical violence, walking out or running away are not the answers. Any of these actions will not change the situation – and could make things worse.

LIFE: THIS WAY

'If I find myself getting wound up, I try to walk away. It's hard sometimes, but often it's not worth the hassle to stay.'

(14-YEAR-OLD GIRL)

What do you do when you're fuming with frustration? Add to the list below!

- **slam doors**
- **go somewhere where no-one can hear you and scream**
- **hoover, clean, or tidy up quickly and with venom**
- **punch a cushion or pillow**
- **go for a walk / run / exercise until you feel better**
- **sing or play favourite music loudly**
- **phone a friend**
- **cry**

Take a break

If you can possibly take a deep breath, you may give yourself time to plan what to do or say next. If you've been refused a request or something has not gone the way you expected, take a step back for a moment. If you're in a discussion, try to end the conversation. Tell the person how you feel: 'I'm really angry / upset / worried at this moment and I need some time to think. I'll come back later.' Try saying something along those lines. Then go and find your own space, and give yourself some thinking time. If you are really worried that the big, red mist of anger is going to descend on you, and you are going to do or say something you may later regret, then get out of the situation fast.

BUT YOU DON'T UNDERSTAND

'When I'm really annoyed I listen to my music dead loud, or take the dog for a long walk.'
(15-YEAR-OLD BOY)

Ask yourself why

First, be kind to yourself and try to understand why you may feel the way you do. Was what happened the last straw at that moment for you? Are you really angry about what has occurred or is it a combination of events leading up to your snapping point? When you give yourself a breather, try to see the problem from both sides; is there another point of view? Are there good reasons why the problem has happened? Perhaps you asked to go out when only the day before you were grounded for coming home late. Maybe you asked your parents for more money than they have at that moment and for something which is not really essential. Or you got a detention for something you know is really your fault.

What is aggression?

Aggression is any behaviour intended to cause physical or emotional pain or damage. The key word here is 'intent'. If the pain is not caused intentionally, then technically it's not aggression. An animal killing another for food is not aggression, it's a necessary action for survival. A very physical football match is an example of channelled aggression, though if the players get out of hand and start losing their tempers rather than playing fairly, then that's aggression! But the actions of a bully, or a gang wrecking a telephone box, is aggression because both are acting with the intention of causing damage one way or another.

Rage

There's so much pressure on people in modern society that people reach breaking point over all manner of things. It could be a long supermarket queue, a late train or a traffic jam. It's very often something which stops you getting on with all the other things you want to fit into a busy life – a delay or an event which doesn't go according to plan or expectations.

Your rage could be due to a build up of frustration. It's true that frustration is more likely to cause aggression if you're not expecting it. In other words, you may cope better with traffic delays, if you've expecting it to be a busy time, say, during rush hour. But you have chosen to travel at that time and so have taken some kind of 'control' over the situation, it was your own decision. Or perhaps you know that leaving late would mean you'd miss the bus, meeting your friends and the start of the film. Could you have prepared to leave earlier? If you plan ahead for any event, a lot of frustration could be avoided.

> *'I hate traffic queues when I'm late, and I hate waiting for other people to pick me up and them being late.'*
>
> (15-YEAR-OLD GIRL)

Unrealistic expectations

It may be that you are meeting someone who is always late. In which case if you plan ahead, you could ask them to meet you half an hour ahead of when you actually need them there. Nobody is perfect, and you will need to make allowances for others. There's an old saying that if you want something done properly, do it yourself. Everyone has loads of things to think about and stuff on their mind at any one time, which may not be of the same priority as your concerns. If you ask someone to do something and they forget, forgive them. And if you forget something, forgive yourself. If you really need to know that something has been done, then either do it yourself or double-check that the other person has remembered in good time.

Here are some ways to remember those things to do:

- Have a calendar in a place where everyone has access (like the kitchen or the hall). Mark on it things like birthdays, events, meetings, appointments and so on. Tell someone in the family when you write something in, just in case they forget to check the calendar!

- Keep a diary or wall-chart.

- Write a yellow sticky note, attach it to your bag, the front door, your parent's forehead ... (You may be planning your day, your parent may be planning the week ahead, their work schedule, child-care arrangements, shopping, bills and social life for the entire family.)

- Put the item that needs mending or cleaning in a place where you'll see it until you get the job done.

- Leave out your kit for the day in a place where you definitely can't avoid it (the stairs is not a brilliantly safe idea, but near the front door may be better).

- Before you leave home, run through a quick mental check of things that need doing (lights off, windows shut, money, house key, and someone knows where you are going). There's nothing more frustrating than taking a video or something back only to find the box is empty and you've made a wasted trip.

What other things work for you?

Not my fault

Thinking that someone is frustrating you on purpose and without good reason can also add to aggressive feelings. You could be right; sometimes people do things just to be aggravating. You'll particularly know this if you have brothers and sisters who may sometimes be awkward simply to wind you up. Be superior, be a better person than they are by not rising to the bait. There is nothing which disarms others more than if you smile sweetly and agree, or just accept what they say – well, for now at least!

Go with the flow

Many philosophers have tried to struggle to find the answer to the meaning of life, and many books have been written, but sometimes there just doesn't seem to be any good reason why things don't go according to plan or your way. You arrange a day out and it rains, your friend goes sick, you lose your money or your parent works late and can't give you a lift. Many things in life will not go according to how we want them. Rather than despair, feel furious, cry with frustration (you can give yourself permission to do any of these if it makes you feel better temporarily!), try to see a way through. Something good may in fact happen: a friend calls who you've wanted to speak to, or an alternative plan works out well. Can you make something better happen out of the problem? Maybe whatever it was, wasn't meant to be; this could apply to little things, as well as fairly major disasters. No one is getting at you. Life hasn't got it in for you: it's just the way it is.

> *'Rugby is my stress reducer. After a good hard game where I've boshed a couple of people, and they've boshed me, I feel much better!'*
> (16-YEAR-OLD BOY)

Response to frustration

Frustration can cause people to react in different ways. It can cause:

- **depression**
- **despair**
- **withdrawal**
- **apathy or tiredness**
- **aggressive thoughts**
- **aggressive behaviour**
- **feelings of uselessness**
- **temper tantrums (return to childhood)**

It can cause all of these at sometime in everyone, depending on the person, how they're feeling and the situation they are in. What's true is that it is very unhealthy to bottle up your feelings. You have to find a way of letting them out, otherwise the results may be disastrous! It's well known, for example, that quiet inoffensive people have exploded and done something they've regretted – even murder – in a moment of madness. They may be the kind of people who normally would never say boo to a goose and take a lot of hassle without reacting externally or doing anything about it. This is a bit like getting a can of pop and shaking it hard for a few hours. When you take the top off ... BOOM! So channel this frustration into something positive like an activity which will take your mind off things for a while and allow you to relax and de-stress. Or talk to someone about how you're feeling and why.

Most likely causes

It's been found that the things most likely to cause aggression and frustration are if:

ARRGN! One piece missing from a 2000 piece jigsaw!

- you're very close to reaching your goal and are stopped just short

You can't go to the disco, it's Nan's birthday! GRRR!

- the thing that's frustrating you seems unfair

I didn't pinch that sausage from your plate!

- you've been accused of something you are not guilty of doing

Frustration – life-long learning

You learn how to cope with frustration all through childhood, from not being fed when you are hungry to being refused to stay up late, so your own reaction pattern is probably set by the time you reach adolescence. In children you usually find that levels of aggression are stable, that is they stay constant. You're probably aware that out of the friends you have there are some who are likely to 'blow up' over the smallest thing. Some people have very

BUT YOU DON'T UNDERSTAND 41

quick tempers which they find hard to control. When these people get angry, it can be very scary, especially if you know they are capable of hurting others. Other people seem to have an endless tolerance and can take a lot of rubbish thrown at them without batting an eyelid. You will also know some people who lose their temper and stay angry or sulk for hours, and others blow up and cool down within minutes.

It all depends on the type of personality and experiences you have had. What's interesting is that those people who get very frustrated and aggressive usually see others as 'against' them. The 'no-one likes me' feeling. These types often resort to bullying, using violence to show they are more powerful than others. The people who cope with frustration better take a different point of view. They seem able to put themselves in other people's shoes and don't take things that happen as a personal insult, and are less likely to feel out of control in difficult circumstances. They may also have a more positive attitude to life and find it easier to problem-solve, rather than being victims of events.

LIFE: THIS WAY

> These are a few of my frustrating things:
>
> 'never having enough money to get what I want.'
>
> 'people who dither when you're in a rush.'
>
> 'people who ram shopping trolleys into the back of your ankles in supermarkets.'
>
> 'getting told off when I haven't done anything wrong.'
>
> 'people not listening to my point of view.'
>
> 'people treating me like a small child.'
>
> 'when my dad says "You'll realise when you're older!" Grrrr!'
>
> 'unfairness.'
>
> 'people who lie and then get away with it.'
>
> (14- and 15-year-olds)

Can you explain all these to me?

I only want a stamp!

And I only want to send a love letter!

POST OFFICE

Living with aggression

Some people live in families where violence is common. The adults in the home use their strength and size to make children or younger people do what they want, or use violence as a punishment for wrong-doings. These adults may also use violence for no reason other than to let out their own frustrations at life. Violence in families is often a pattern handed down through generations. The adults were violent to their children, the children grow up and knowing violence as a means of control repeat that pattern to their children, and so it goes on.

> 'Before I started school, I used to play at my friend's. One day she did some little thing wrong and I wondered why she started to cry. Then I saw her dad taking off his belt. I didn't know what was going on, then he started to hit her with it. I ran out of there as fast as I could, screaming my head off, absolutely horrified.'
> (14-YEAR-OLD GIRL)

What is unacceptable?

Many children will have been smacked at some time in their lives for doing something naughty. There are some countries now where even a smack is against the law. But if you suffer more than a smack, if you are beaten or punched or the smackings are regular occurrences, then this is an unacceptable situation. If the fear of violence is as terrifying as the bruises, then this is a problem which must be stopped. There is no excuse for physical punishment. You may have been told you deserve it, you are bad or wicked or stupid. You may think you provoked the situation by your behaviour, there may be lots of problems in your home which the family believes are excuses for violent behaviour.

> *'I agree with research that's been done. I think TV violence can have an affect on people, especially children. I think copycat violence would be reduced if they took it off TV, and if adults were more careful about what they let younger children see.'*
> (15-YEAR-OLD GIRL)

But there are no excuses for violent behaviour, not for any family member, not for any reason. Everyone has the right to feel safe, whether in their home or on the street. It is not your fault if you are a victim of violence and aggression, and you need to tell someone you can trust. If the person giving the grief at home promises they will change, they probably can't without help. There may be other problems such as drugs, drink, lack of money or psychological ones which need to be looked at first.

What to do

Whatever the problem, it probably won't go away unless some action is taken by one of the people involved: a member of the family may frighten themselves by their extreme behaviour and promise to change. But that change is unlikely without some expert help. You may feel disloyal by telling someone outside of the family about the problem: you may fear the violent person's reactions or the possible break-up of the family. But adults often need help to manage their behaviour, to be shown and to learn how to control their anger and improve their situation. It is not easy for a younger person to take the initiative for making sure those with the problem are helped to become whole. But what is the alternative? If you don't do something, who else will?

Who to ask for help

You must get help, to do this, you will have to share the problem...

tell a teacher at school ...

   a family social worker ...

      a police officer ...

         a doctor ...

           a helpline ...

or anyone you know you can trust who will help.

Be honest about the problem, think carefully about what you are going to say (there are people who will exaggerate or lie about the real issues in order to gain attention – this could lead to big trouble for all concerned). Do not exaggerate, and stick to the facts, but do not make the problem seem smaller than it is if it's really quite intolerable. Telling someone will not mean that immediately the family will be split up or people are arrested. There are many ways in which organisations and support workers can help families with managing their anger, and achieve better communication in non-aggressive ways.

46 LIFE: THIS WAY

4

BUT YOU DON'T UNDERSTAND

Chapter 4
JUST A PHYSICAL ATTRACTION?

Natter! Natter! Natter! Natter! Natter! Natter!

Friendship

What makes a good friendship?

> 'Me and my best friend have been mates for over six years. We first met in year 7. We're always there for each other and we're always gossiping. We're able to talk about anything to each other without getting embarrassed. We also talk about problems and help each other through the bad times.'
>
> (16-YEAR-OLD GIRL)

> *'Although I don't have any best friends any more, what keeps the friends I have friends, is that we all share similar interests. This mostly includes football and a shared interest in cars, especially high-powered ones.'*
>
> (17-YEAR-OLD BOY)

As you go through life, you may find that you have many of different kinds of friendships. There may be people you sit next to in class, or work with, or belong to the same club or group activity who you get on well with but don't see outside of that environment. There may be friends you see often, and friends (perhaps who live a long way from you) whom you only see occasionally. There may be one or two special close friends with whom you would share everything and who may remain friends forever. It's also quite normal to lose touch with some friends or to grow out of the friendship as you both mature and change. Don't feel bad if you find you no longer have as much in common with a special friend as you once did.

What makes a close friendship?

For any friendship to develop you must be prepared to share yourself and your thoughts and feelings. If you put on an act to impress or to try to make people like you, others will soon see the real you when they get to know you better. If you never talk about yourself, you'll find it hard to make close friends – how can others get to know what you have in common if you don't give an opinion or share your thoughts? On the other hand, talk about yourself too much and you'll put other people off!

Close friendships usually have many of these qualities:

- **respect**
- **reliability**
- **sharing**
- **experiences**
- **trust**
- **similar life**
- **listening**
- **responding**
- **understanding**
- **laughter**
- **communication**
- **being there when needed**
- **equality**
- **helping**
- **same interests**
- **honesty**

Being a friend

What other qualities are important to your friendships? What would your ideal friend be like? Make a list. From that list, tick off the qualities you have in your friendships, and add any more. Do you make a good friend to others?

Sharing the loneliness

There will be times when you may feel very alone. Thoughts are spinning around in your head and you can't seem to find answers. It really can help to have someone to talk to. A problem shared really can be a problem halved. Human beings are group people but some find it easier than others to enjoy being part of a group. Most people like to be sociable, to have a laugh, to share good times and bad. It is great if you have a friend who you can call or hang around with when you don't want to be alone.

So how can you find new friends if you've just moved to a new school or a new area and you've left your good friends behind? Or if you find it difficult to make friendships? Take a look at yourself.

Make a list of your qualities, and see if there's anything you'd like to improve and could do something about. Making that first contact with someone and giving a good impression can be very important. Do you say 'hello' to others first? Do you smile back if someone looks at you, or even smile first? Often the first step to a friendship is that opening statement which begins a conversation, and it will often be to do with a shared experience; this could range from 'This homework is hard' or 'Why is the bus late?' to anything which requires a response from the other person.

Then you've got to do a little more work to keep the conversation going. So listen to what the other person replies and see if you can respond accordingly. If you can make a person laugh, even better as it will make you seem fun to be with. If you can find out something you have in common (where you live, who you know, what activities you like to do) then you may have found the opportunity to see that person or chat with them again.

Finding a friend

First impressions are so important and people like to fit in and be part of an acceptable group. Is there anything about you which is different from most others? Are you clean and presentable in appearance? Do you slouch or frown? Do you avoid eye-contact and making conversation? Can you do anything about these things? Maybe you like to be really wacky and dress and behave differently from others.

If I changed my hairstyle would you be my friend

Pong!

Actually, your hair is fine – a bath might help though!

This is great as long as you are happy and comfortable being you. Many people will like you for being different, and if you are happy, you will be confident and shouldn't have much trouble finding good friends. If you are physically different in some way, then confidence again is the key. Don't be afraid to join in, to make the best of your abilities, to find others in similar situations. If you have different or less common interests (hang-gliding, glass-painting, learning Russian) there will be group or organisation of like-minded people with whom you can get in touch.

You will then meet people who have the same interests and enthusiasm, and that's a good starting point for a friendship. So if you are new to an area or your best friend has moved on, check out where you can meet some new people. Look at school or work noticeboards, local papers,

I've always wanted to try skateboarding, can we meet up sometime?

libraries, on the Internet, 'phone book ... Ask an adult who knows the local area. You will find everything from art activities, to sports, from drama to youth organisations, from differently abled groups to music going on in your area. Making friends takes a little effort, you will need to find out about an activity, make that 'phone call, and then turn up at a meeting to get your foot in the friendship door.

Liking some people more than others

Many people say it's love that makes the world go round. If this is true then it's 'liking' that keeps it spinning. For a lot of us close relationships with our family and some of our friends are very important for our happiness. As humans we all have a basic need to be with other people.

So what is it that makes us choose to be close to some people and not others?

What is liking?

Liking someone is when you think about them in a positive way as a person, even when you know their strengths and weaknesses. Loving (and this is true with very close friends, too) is a more intense liking and is usually made up of three elements:

- Attachment: the need to be with the person and emotional support.

- Caring: a feeling of concern and responsibility.

- Intimacy: sharing private thoughts and feelings with the person more than with anyone else.

As well as the above three elements, there is another attached to loving someone as a partner – in the girl / boy sense – and that is of physical loving and being attracted to someone in a sexually intimate way. Men and women don't need to be in love to want to have sex with each other, but for a true loving relationship all of the four elements will probably be there.

More about love in Chapter 5

> 'Me and my best friend have been best friends for an age. I think the 'glue' that holds us together is the fact that we both know when we need each other and when we need time apart. We share the same interests and love doing everything together. But when we argue it doesn't last long because we both need each other too much!'
>
> (17-YEAR-OLD GIRL)

Women and girls report when surveyed 'loving' their friends more than men and boys do, or claim to do! This may be because girls' friendships tend to be closer than those of many boys. Girls are more likely to tell each other close secrets and go out together a lot, spending more time with each other. Girls also use more 'mental' communication, with much more chat and conversation about absolutely everything. Boys and men tend to have more 'surface' and physical level communication. Their conversations are for more likely to be centred around common interests like sports, hobbies, music and so on, and many friendships are based around group activities like sports. Maybe males feel it is not manly to share their hopes and fears with others.

Changing relationships

There's no doubt that relationships and friendships change over time and we can expect this to happen. Those that become one-sided often don't last long. What's probably true is that friendships and relationships do pass through a series of phases a bit like the ones below:

1. Things that you have in common with the other person will be important, and may determine whether or not you meet up in the first place. Examples of these things that are similar to you both may be:

- **your age**
- **your sex**
- **religion**
- **level of attractiveness**
- **interests**
- **clubs you belong to**
- **social class**
- **class at school**
- **culture**
- **where you live**
- **lifestyle**
- **have a boy/girlfriend**

So to some extent your choice of friends is really made for you. Where you live, how you look and the things you do reduce the number of people available for you to meet. Those people you do meet have almost been pre-selected. Most often they'll also be from your own ethnic, racial, religious and educational groups. Because they are similar to you and have things in common, you have something to talk about and communication is made easier. At this first stage then, attraction to some people rather than others has little to do with your own choice.

You like what you know and can understand: people and things that are predictable. Even at this stage, though, you may start to weed out those that you definitely don't want to choose as friends. For example, some people can be too familiar and perhaps begin to suffocate you. The more you see them the more you realise you don't want to see them. For any friendship to be successful, there has to have a 'setting down of rules'. Anyone who gets too close for comfort too soon is unlikely to become your friend, as you'll probably need time to build up trust. Someone who comes into your life very quickly may make you suspicious that they could also leave just as fast, leaving behind a gaping hole.

2. This stage involves your personality and attitudes. You are more likely to be friends with someone who shares your beliefs and has a similar personality so that you can enjoy doing the same things together.

> *'The reason why me and my friends have stuck together for so long is because we have so many things in common. We don't spend all our time together, though. We don't have a 'leader' in our group and no-one feels better than anyone else. We're treated equally which has worked for us.'*
> (16-YEAR-OLD BOY)

Someone who agrees with us helps to give us more self-confidence in our own thoughts and opinions. It's true that:

- anyone who shares the same views as you, you see as intelligent and sensitive.

- people who agree about things generally find it easier to talk to each other.

- it's also flattering when someone pays you a compliment and seems to like you (it's a kind of a reward).

> ### Strange, but true!
> Someone who starts off by disliking you and then comes to like you will be liked more than someone who likes us from the start. Following this? Someone who starts off by liking you and then dislikes you will be disliked more than someone who disliked you from the start!!

3. People that complement each other (in other words, are able to see exactly what the other person needs) and relationships or friendships that give rewards are the ones that last the longest. Your feelings for your friends can be seen as the amount of reward you get from the relationship and how much you have to put in (how much it costs you emotionally).

If the rewards are great and the costs low, the greater the attraction and the longer you are likely to stay together. Giving and receiving are very important, as is getting a fair deal out of the friendship. There's a belief that we're all basically selfish, getting as much out of a relationship as possible.

People whose relationships last tend to be more alike in terms of age, intelligence, education and career plans as well as physical attractiveness.

> 'Me and Gemma have been best friends since I moved here when I was 7. I had to start a new school and Gemma was given the job of looking after me on my first day. We've been friends ever since. We're very close but have other friends and boyfriends so don't live in each other's pockets which is probably why we're still friends. We're very honest with each other and have the same sense of humour and I know what she's thinking most of the time without her telling me. We're on the same wavelength and it's good to be friends after so long. This year we're off on holiday together!'
>
> (17-YEAR-OLD GIRL)

Strange, but true!

If you don't like someone, they probably don't like you and vice versa. That might seem obvious, but think about it next time you are pretending to be nice to someone you really dislike!

Instinct

When you first meet someone, you often rely on your instinct to guess whether this is a person you are going to like and trust. Sometimes you may take an instant dislike at a first meeting, even though you can't voice exactly what it is you don't like. You might find it valuable to keep that little voice of concern in the back of your mind. You may get to know, like and gradually trust the person. Perhaps they are a friend of a good friend of yours, and you want to see and like in them what your friend likes. However, as you go through life you may find that the person you met who with your 'sixth sense' didn't feel right actually lets you down quite badly at a later date. You may find yourself saying 'You know, I never was sure about them!'

Friendships need work

A good friendship is also about give and take. It should not always be you who does the calling, the arranging or the sorting out to meet. If you find it always seems to be you who gets in touch with your friend, ask yourself why that might be. You could try leaving it a while and see if they actually call you. We want to be wanted. We don't want to be wanted just for what we can give or do for the other person. It's back to 'rewards'.

Does your friend actually listen to what you are saying and respond? Or do they seem to talk over you or change the subject completely when you are really wanting to hear some advice or opinion on what you have just said?

Does your friend make you feel good? Or do they seem to criticise you – perhaps to boost their own self-esteem? If your friendship is not a two-way thing, if it ever makes you feel bad, if your friend lets you down badly without good reason on more than one occasion, ask yourself if that person really is a friend. It could be time to let that friendship fade away and find someone new.

Falling out

If you've fallen out with a friend or you feel you may have let them down, then what can you do? Well, you may need to apologise (or whatever is appropriate) or you may want them to say sorry to you. So you'll need to be in touch, whether in person, via a letter, e-mail, or on the 'phone. Some friends may end up having a really big row, which clears up all the misunderstandings and may even bring them closer together as they realise that their friendship can survive tough times. If you cannot resolve your difference or the problem, then maybe the friendship was not as strong as you thought. Let it go. If you have done all you honestly can to make it work and to clear the air, then that's all that could be done. Don't waste time making life unpleasant for them and yourself; it's not worth it! Do not feel guilty. Move on.

The truth is that we all seek out friends, and there are some people that we like more than others. There will also be friends for different situations, and of varying degrees of closeness. When this liking of a particular friend grows, we can also fall in love, as we see in the next chapter ...

60 | LIFE: THIS WAY

BUT YOU DON'T UNDERSTAND

Chapter 5
DO YA LOVE ME?

What is love?

The word 'love' means different things to different people and it is hard to define in any relationship, let alone one. Most mothers feel an overwhelming sense of love when they give birth to a baby. If you live within a family, and have a good experience, then you will know the kind of love you have for parents and siblings and they for you. We also use the word 'love' when we really mean 'like' for all sorts of things and experiences. It is not an easy emotion to describe. We know what pain feels like, and sadness and anger, fear and hate. But love: does it really exist? Nearly everyone just assumes it does, but trying to figure out what it means is very difficult because it means different things to different people.

> *'The first time I fell in love, it felt really special. I smiled every time I thought of him or saw him. I looked forward to every time I saw him. I knew I was in love as my heart skipped a beat whenever I thought of him.'*
> (17-YEAR-OLD GIRL)

You may laugh at it, at first. After all how could anyone love someone enough to die for them or put them above all else, let alone share their toothbrush. What must it be like to have such a head-over-heels, smack-in-the-face, blissful love? There are all sorts of kinds of love which can be experienced in many different ways.

Perfect love

Most people know love in different senses, like the way you love your family. One kind of love is almost 'perfect' and is the kind which you feel for someone you don't know at all, like an actor or singer. It's perfect, because the chances of you actually getting to know that person in real life, and discover that they are human is quite remote. If you love someone from afar, they can never let you down. As you grow through the teenage years your mind and body will be preparing for all sorts of emotions and experiences. Many people's first taste of feeling grown up love is by adoring a pop star or actor. You may really feel emotion for that person, yearn to see and talk to them. Feel that you would really get on if you met, and that they would like you too if only they had the chance to talk with you. You may spend a lot of time, money and energy getting to know as much about that person as you can; buying records, magazines, cinema or concert tickets.

Some people will go to their favourite star's home or where the famous person is planned to appear in an effort to actually see and be close to them. This perfect love is really a kind of adoration, but it can feel very real at the time, with all the hurt, sadness and longing that other kinds of love may bring.

As your tastes change, you may lose interest in the particular person you admired, or you may like them always. But you'll become a 'fan' rather than someone who is obsessed and cannot function in normal life. This kind of love is not real, but built on a fantasy.

Infatuation and crushes

As well as the fanatical fan type of love described above, many people go through a phase where they feel they are in love with someone a little closer to home. This could be a person you know and admire, and are actually in contact with, whether daily or from time to time. It's absolutely normal, and once again it is most likely your hormones and emotions having a practice ready for knowing the real thing at a later date. There are a couple of differences between this kind of love and the fan or perfect type.

Because you know or can be in contact with the person, it is less of a fantasy, and your imagination can see more hopes of your dream turning into reality. The other difference is that it is much more likely to have a sexual base. When you are a teenager, you may not yet know whether you are going to be heterosexual as an adult (physically / sexually attracted to members of the opposite sex) or homosexual (physically / sexually attracted to people of the same sex as yourself). Most people will have a definite idea, but some remain unsure even into adulthood. However, it is perfectly normal to be infatuated, or have a crush on a person of the same sex, even if you later grow up to be confidently heterosexual.

The dangers of crushes

The person you may have a crush on could be a teacher, a group leader, a family friend or even a friend of the same age. But usually the object of your attention is an adult. In a way, it's a little like perfect love, because there are probably good reasons why that person will never be able to love you back. This may be because of the age difference, the job that they do or because they are already happily married. Try to see this love for what it is. It's a dream, it's a practice for the real thing. You may find yourself thinking and dreaming of the object of your affection, hanging around trying to catch a glimpse of them, keeping something they have touched. This is normal and it's okay.

But if you ever go beyond the dreaming and thinking, it will most likely end in tears and trouble. If you ever let this person know how you feel, at best you could be rejected and made to feel small; at worst, it could put the person in a seriously awkward position. It has been known, for example, for teachers to have relationships with mature-looking pupils. This kind of relationship could be against that person's job code of conduct; it could also be against the law if it developed into a physical and sexual relationship and the younger person is under the age of 16. The younger person is also less likely to be able to cope with the emotions and trauma of the situation, and things could get really out of hand. Life could become difficult for both people involved. If you find yourself besotted with someone you know you cannot have, just understand it for what it is. It's not real love.

Physical attraction

As you grow and your hormones start to run riot, you may spend quite a lot of your time thinking, daydreaming, dreaming and maybe chatting to your friends about physical love and sex. This is really normal. Sex is meant to be attractive to us. Your body is preparing you to grow up and make babies. If people stopped being interested in sex, then that would bring an abrupt end to the human race. Think about it! The difference between us and other creatures is that our brains allow us to make choices and decisions. We can think things through, where other species just do what comes instinctively and naturally like birds nesting every spring. At the root base of our later choice in a partner may be a subconscious desire to continue the human race. Which is why you are often at first physically attracted to a person's body as well as later their mind and personality. It's nature's way of telling you that they will make a good breeding partner for you!

But because we are human beings in a modern world, with longer life spans and more complications than our distant forebears, we need to make intelligent decisions about our partners. Especially if we hope to stay with that person for a very long time, perhaps even for marriage and life.

Take a look back at the 'What is liking?' section in Chapter 4. A mature loving relationship will contain all of those four elements of attraction and liking. Someone once said that true love was where both people had 'equality and individuality, respect for each other, trusting the other person 110%, and fancying them even if they were sitting on the loo'! If you find yourself in a relationship where, like friendship, you are not getting the rewards you would want, think again – it may be more of an addictive kind of love or lust than real love.

Well, you didn't give me time to do myself up!

If it hurts, then is it really love?

If you find yourself 'in love' with someone who doesn't really want you or is not interested in you, then this is not real love either. Real love is when someone wants you as much as you want them – it has that sharing equality. How do you know it's real love? Well, you're can't be in love with:

- someone you don't really know or who doesn't know you, like an actor or the guy at the bus stop.

- the way someone looks or how much money they have. It's what's on the inside that counts.

- someone just because everyone else thinks they're great. It's what you think! This can work the other way, too, and you may be put off someone you do really like because your family or friends don't like them.

- anyone if you can't accept their faults, or they yours, or accept them at their worst or in times of trouble.

- someone if you have to put on a show and behave the way you think they want you to and hide the real you.

You may think that if this person really got to know you, then things could work out. You may think someone who behaves very badly towards you can change, and they may promise to. But if you are not getting anything back from the relationship, and if you find yourself sad, in pain and unhappy, then remember that you deserve better.

Oh Chaz, he stood me up for the third time in a row!

He really isn't worth it. You deserve better, someone with a great personality.

Like you Chaz!?

Many books have been written for adults about relationships, love and psychology, about how to make things better, work out and so on. Some are terribly interesting and useful, and if you want to know more about yourself and others' behaviour, check out your library or bookshop. Some people fall into relationship traps where probably both partners know they are making each other unhappy, but they may not have the skill, life experiences or confidence to know how to break away from each other. Adults often find themselves repeating the experiences of their parents in case where perhaps their home life was violent or one of the partners had a drink or drugs problem. The child grows up, and finds a partner similar to their background experiences as it's what they know. This is more of an addictive kind of love, and most addictions are not good for you. Addictive love, the kind where you just seemed hooked into a person who you know does not make you happy and probably never will, needs courage and confidence to break away from. A victim may need counselling of some kind to re-build their confidence and belief in themselves. You deserve the best.

Lust isn't love either!

Lust, whereby the only feeling you have for the other person is a physical attraction, isn't love either. You may feel hormonally charged up about someone, but if you got to know the person you were lusting after, you would soon find that apart from physical attraction there is nothing else there which is going to turn into a relationship which has a closeness and friendship at its base. Most teenage relationships start off with lust! These are the friendships which last two days or two weeks. Two people are going out / dating / seeing each other exclusively one week and enemies the next.

These short-lived relationships are totally normal. Once again, they are practice runs for the real thing. By getting to know someone a little better, you find out that they may not be right for you.

This is why many people go out for months or years, really getting to know and understand each other before making a life-long commitment like marriage. The dating games which go on when you are at school, college or even at work form a huge part of the social scene. There are loads of rules to this game, and anyone who breaks the rules of the group majority is in for a hard time! There may be rules about exclusivity, cheating on someone, fancying the same person your friend does, dating someone your friends hate, sleeping around (or so people suspect) and so on. There are loads of do's and don'ts, so be careful out there if you want to keep the peace amongst your friends and family, and keep respect for yourself.

She looked gorgeous, but it turns out she hates almost everything I like from footy, to my best mate, to pets!

Lucky escape!

Bad love

Sex is illegal for anyone under the age of 16 years in the United Kingdom, which means it is against the law of the land. The idea is that people under this age may not be physically or mentally mature enough to cope with a sexual relationship, and so the law is there for your protection. If you decide to break the law, then you must think of the consequences which include getting into trouble with the police and your family, the risk of pregnancy and sexually transmitted diseases, and having regrets yourself.

You have the right to say no to sex until you meet someone you really care for, or when the time is right for you.

Sex is also illegal if it is incest, when close members of a family, like brother and sister, or a parent and child, have sexual relations. This is not love. This is sexual abuse, as is anything done to you of a sexual nature with which you do not agree and have not consented. If you find yourself in such a situation, then know that you could be physically and emotionally hurt. You must get help and advice. There is lots available. Check out the index. Don't try to handle these seriously upsetting situations alone.

SEE THE INDEX SECTION ON WHERE TO GO FOR ADVICE AND HELP!

Meantime, back to the dating game!

What things do you look for in a partner? Take a look at the following list and pick out the three most important things you would like to find in your ideal person to go out with:

- **attractive**
- **mature**
- **honest**
- **money**
- **patient**

- **considerate**
- **reliable**
- **sense of humour**
- **physically fit**
- **intelligent**

- **hardworking**
- **good manners**
- **kind**
- **romantic**
- **popular**

> Lives locally ✓
> Attractive ✓
> Like exercise ✓
> Smells good ✓
> Same breed ✓
> Likes same kind of lamp-post and food ✓

Add to that list any other qualities you'd like to find, and when you go out with someone, make a mental note of the good things they have and compare them with those you would like to find. Remember that no-one is perfect, and that romance in novels and films does not usually reflect reality! To be truly happy with someone, the good times and their good points must outweigh any bad ones.

Pressure

It's generally true that girls usually begin to take an interest in boys earlier than boys become attracted to girls. Girls usually mature physically and mentally earlier than boys. As boys' and girls' personalities are so different, it can help to form friendships with members of the opposite sex quite early on if you are in a mixed sex school. Not 'going out' friendships, but just friendships. In this way everyone can benefit from the exchange of thoughts and ideas. Sometimes people who go to single sex schools have very little experience of members of the opposite sex and lack confidence in forming friendships. Boys and girls, men and women, can be platonic and lifelong friends without wanting to be sexual partners.

When you do start going out with someone and begin a relationship there's a whole new world of pressures waiting to drop on your head.

Boys may feel:

- they can't be themselves with girls//
- they have to live up to the expectations of others
- girls expect far too much
- they have to be cool and not show they're nervous
- pressure from friends, asking what you've done, how far you've gone, and so on
- hurried: people start pairing you off
- there's no time and space to find out about each other
- they are expected to 'pull', or have a girlfriend.

> 'What I would consider to be my first real kiss happened in a cinema in America. After what felt like a lifetime of waiting and wondering what kissing someone you really love and who also loves you, would feel like, I decided the time was right. (Even though she had a brace and I was at an awkward angle due to the cinema seats.) It felt good. Maybe not as good as I'd imagined it to be, but I still got a strange tingling up my spine. I felt happy in the knowledge that I'd had the courage to go through with it.'
>
> (17-YEAR-OLD BOY)

Girls may feel:

- most boys only want one thing
- boys expect you to go along with them and what they want to do
- they're expected to have boyfriends
- they're expected to behave in a stereotyped way
- they're not expected to make the first move
- boys watch every move they make
- they can't be true to themselves and show their true feelings
- they have to dress or look a certain way.

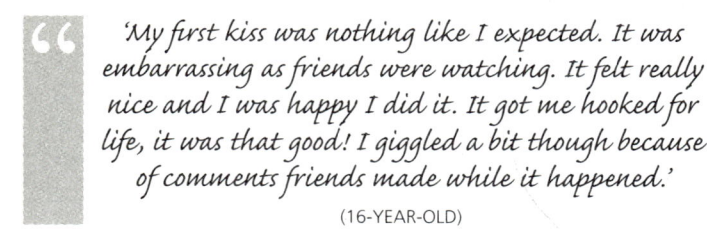

> *'My first kiss was nothing like I expected. It was embarrassing as friends were watching. It felt really nice and I was happy I did it. It got me hooked for life, it was that good! I giggled a bit though because of comments friends made while it happened.'*
>
> (16-YEAR-OLD)

Sex and life

Many relationships build slowly and gradually: the couple become good friends, getting to know each other and becoming close mentally and then perhaps physically. Many other young people are keen to explore the physical side sooner rather than later, and sex crops up as an issue. Do you or don't you? The most important thing to remember at this time, is never to do anything you don't want to do. Never be pressurised into anything you know you're not ready for and that goes for all things whether they're sexual or not!

Think about the following:

- Sex once given, cannot be taken back.

- Moral aspects: some cultures and religions believe that remaining a virgin until after marriage is very important. How guilty would you feel, or what trouble could you cause if you disobey your life background beliefs?

- A virgin is a person who has not had full sexual intercourse.

- Giving the most intimate part of yourself to someone else should be a thought-out loving and valued (by both) experience. It should feel 'right' and without guilt.

- Everyone does not 'do it', despite what they might claim. If you want to wait until you are sure, that is your right and choice.

Sex needs to be discussed between the two of you. Some couples want to take things slowly, especially if they're both young with their whole lives before them, or they plan to save a full sexual relationship until after marriage. This is no problem for the couple if they both agree. Other couples believe sex and intimacy is an important part of their relationship as a special closeness, and believe they're mature enough to handle it. It just depends on you, your circumstances, how much you feel about the other person and what you eventually decide. There is plenty of exploring of each other's bodies which can be enjoyed without having to 'go all the way' and have full penetrative sex. Whilst many teenagers are sexually active, others decide to wait until the time is exactly right for them. 'Those who say most, do least' can be a true saying. This statement can apply to almost anything you hear someone boasting about!

Protection

If you do decide an active sex life is right for you, then there are a few important things to consider. The main one is risk. Pregnancy or sexually transmitted diseases, such as genital herpes or Aids are real dangers to be considered.

The safest way to protect yourself is obviously not to have sex! This could also be by not getting into a situation you may find it difficult to get out of (for example, getting drunk at a party and not being able to think clearly). The next safest is sticking to one partner. The more partners you have the more chance you have of catching a sexually transmitted disease. Using condoms, although not 100% safe also significantly reduces the dangers.

You can get confidential help about contraception from your doctor or your local Family Planning Clinic.

There's a room free upstairs. Go on, you know you've fancied me for ages!

Hic, I feel sick...the room's all fuzzy...

Beware, Shaz, you might catch something!

Sex = love?

Sex isn't the same thing as love in the true sense of the word. Sex can be self-centred and a purely physical and selfish craving. There are people who see the opposite sex as just 'bodies' to be used. Don't deceive yourself into thinking that people really care for you when all they want is sex. The truth is that they probably don't care for you as much as you would like. Hormones are flying high in the teenage years, people feel they want to experiment. There is a lot of pressure and gossip amongst groups as to who has 'done it', when and with whom. Boys in particular may try to blackmail girls into having sex and will try every trick and persuasive argument they can think of. Don't be conned into doing something you may later regret. Respect yourself and your own body. Take no notice of pressure from other people. It is your decision alone.

If you don't want to, you don't have to and if you are under 16 years, you are under the age of consent and full sex is against the law. Listen to Uncle Baz, you know it makes sense!

UNCLE BAZ

Living up to expectations

Perhaps some people think that by having sex they'll feel more grown up and be able to boast about it to others. Perhaps there is pressure amongst a group of friends to be one of the 'in' crowd. But if any of your friends are using it as some kind of 'status symbol', then you need to ask yourself how well they are actually handling the emotions and responsibility that goes with a decision of this sort. Boys especially try to live up to the expectations of their friends and may boast about going further with a girl than they actually did. This, in turn, makes others feel that they need to get a girlfriend so they don't get left out in the sexual stakes.

The first time you make love with someone will be remembered all your life. It's up to you what that experience will be like. Will it be in an alcoholic blur or somewhere scutty with someone you weren't that keen on anyway? Or will it be worth remembering? If you sleep with more than one partner, do you risk being called a 'slag', 'slut', 'tart' or any of the other stereotyped names? Be proud of your body, don't give it to anybody, and take pride in your decisions.

Sex is a very important issue and the way you deal with it will, in part, set the pattern for this part of your life and for future relationships.

Religious views

Many religions still maintain that sex is only morally right when you're in a marriage. Neither a man or a woman should have sex before they get married and many cultures believe that this makes for mutual respect, faithfulness and true love. Any other form of sex outside marriage is said to affect the personalities of the people involved and will decrease the stability and happiness of the marriage.

There is masses of information available about sex and making love, from teen mags to television, books to leaflets to advice lines. There are all sort of myths which fly around, such as you can't get pregnant the first time you have sex, or whilst a girl is having a period. Or really stupid statements like 'Trust me, you know I'll be careful', or 'Don't you like me? You'd do it if you really cared for me'. Stories and statements like these are not true. Don't believe everything you may hear from friends unless you know the real facts.

BAZ'S Thought for the day:
Be careful, be wise, be sensible, be happy!

LIFE: THIS WAY

Chapter 6
DUMPSVILLE!

Rejection

Everyone feels rejected at some time or another and we all have to learn how to cope. How well you manage affects how you feel about yourself and how others see you. You may face lots of different types of rejection in one day from getting ignored by a sales assistant, to being turned down for the job you really wanted. Make a list of the rejections that you feel have affected you and think about how you coped.

Experiences might include things like:

- **not getting into a sports team**
- **failing an audition**
- **being refused a cuddle by a parent**
- **a friend not turning up for a meeting**
- **an adult not listening**
- **a relationship break-up**
- **someone not phoning when they said they would**
- **not being included in an outing**

Did you handle the situation well or badly? Did you learn from the experience?

> *'I found rejection surprisingly easy to cope with. I was going through a particularly nasty part of my life and it just seemed to fit in with everything else. I got through by mainly listening to loud aggressive music, and convincing myself that someone better would come along. At the same time, I found it very difficult to accept the relationship was over. But it didn't hit me half as hard as one of my friends when they were dumped.'*
>
> (17-YEAR-OLD BOY)

Feelings

You may go through different feelings when you are rejected, especially in a relationship. If this has ever happened to you, there's a probability that you felt at least one of the following:

- **desperate**
- **miserable**
- **hurt**
- **uninteresting**
- **small**
- **angry**

- **left out**
- **wanting to cry all the time**
- **wrenching in your stomach**
- **useless**
- **there's something wrong with you**

- **sadness**
- **depressed**
- **tense**
- **stupid**
- **lonely**

The negative trap

The fear of rejection and isolation can be the cause of great suffering when you're a teenager. Group friendships can be incredibly complicated with friends falling in and out of favour sometimes on a daily basis. One day you are best friends with someone, the next they are not speaking to you. The same can happen in partner relationships too, especially those formed when you are still young and at school. You want to be liked, valued and accepted for being you. Sometimes to achieve this you have to change your behaviour a little and compromise. Once you've felt rejected, you hurt for a while and then reach a point where you realise you have to pick yourself up, dust yourself off and get on with life. If this happens it will probably help to try and turn the rejection into something positive. Perhaps:

- you realise you hadn't that much in common with the person who rejected you

- you're better off without them

- it's someone else's loss for not giving you the opportunity – you would've been great!

- you know you've grown as a result of the experience

- you have to accept, however hard it feels, that life is not always fair

- there's something better around the corner.

Surviving rejection can certainly make you a stronger person, so don't fall into the 'negative thought' trap. Be aware that you may sometimes think negative thoughts; push them away as soon as they start, or get them in perspective. You may see a change in the way you feel about situations that used to get you down.

Consider the following statements:

'I've been rejected so many times for jobs, I'm starting to wonder if it's worth bothering.'

Yes, it is! Everyone fails sometimes. If you never apply for jobs, you have no chance of getting one. Don't give up. You need to think of each situation as completely separate and new, not part of a pattern. Each interview is a brand new opportunity and a new chance.

'My friends always leave me. There's no use making new ones because they will too.'

How do you know till you try? Let things spin out naturally. Have a good look at what went wrong. Is there anything you could have done? If not, be yourself and enjoy each friendship that comes along. Eventually you'll find someone who likes you for being you, so keep smiling, and keep trying.

'Me and my partner are finished and it's my fault!'

Not necessarily. Remember there are two people in a relationship. The blame may not be all yours. Although you're hurting now, try to learn from the experience. Was it really as great as you thought, or are you just remembering the good bits? Think about any bad times you had, maybe that person was not really right for you in the long run.

'I asked her out and she turned me down flat.'

So? No is no, move on. It's not the end of the world and you shouldn't be put off asking other people you like.

'He said I had no brain, just like some of the teachers used to say.'

> *He's turned me down. - I've been rejected!*
>
> *Oh well, HIS loss!*

What do other people know? Sometimes people use attack as their best form of defence. Is there anything not perfect about the person who said it? You know yourself best. Don't think badly of yourself and the chances are other people won't either – the ones that matter, anyway.

'My mate broke up with his girl, and said a lot of bad things about her, and now they are going out again. I don't know what to think. I don't like her.'

There may be times when you don't like the partner your friend has chosen. And you may not think he's made a good choice and it will all end in tears. But sometimes people in a relationship see things through rose-tinted spectacles and can only see the nice bits. All you can do is be there for them through the good times and bad. What you should never do is interfere or bad-mouth their choice, as you risk losing your friendship. Keep a low profile and try not to say 'I told you so' if it all goes wrong. If your friend finds out he's made a mistake, it doesn't help to have it rubbed in.

'I told some of my mates I'm gay, and now half of them aren't speaking to me.'

Yes, but half of them are, and they are your real friends. If the others have a problem, that is their loss. For some of them, it may have been a shock, and perhaps an experience they have not come across before. Hold your head up high, rise above any taunts, and give them a little time. If they don't come around or apologise, move on. You will find new friends to take their place.

'I'm so worried about what other people think of me.'

Don't be: it's what you think that counts. True friends will always think well of you, or forgive you and so will your close family. Make a list of all your good points, and of all the things you have achieved, and give yourself a pat on the back. Remind yourself over and again about the best bits of you, the more you can remind yourself, the higher your confidence and self-esteem will be.

'My best friend's boyfriend was cheating on her with another friend, but now she's ignoring me!'

Give her a little time to get over the hurt and shock. You probably got innocently caught up in the cross-fire of friends being angry with each other. She probably just wants to get mad with someone, and you are closest. Stay out of the complicated mess until she realises she needs a good friend more than a lying boyfriend.

Breaking up is hard to do

What about long-term relationships? Why do they break down? There are many ideas on this.

- **Gender**. Boys and girls see different problems in a relationship. Girls usually report more problems going on, perhaps because they're more sensitive to this than boys. Boys and girls also start relationships with different sets of expectations. The expectations of boys tend to be met more easily than those of girls. Problems reported tend to be things like:

  - different moral values
  - not talking/communicating
  - different expectations
  - general unhappiness
  - lack of sympathy or understanding
  - forgetting something important to the other person
  - not sharing
  - little in common
  - different priorities
  - lack of romance

- **Time factor**. The longer boys and girls have known each other before the relationship started, the more likely the relationship is to last (generally speaking).

- **Arguments**. Some kind of conflict is practically guaranteed in any relationship. It's part of the learning process about relationships. It's the way you get through them that counts! If you approach a problem in a positive way, then it can help the relationship to grow and become even stronger. The important thing is how the arguments are handled. But if you can re-build communication, perhaps when you have had angry words and are not speaking, you will be learning about compromise and give and take. If arguments occur increasingly frequently and about the same thing, doubts may creep into your mind about your relationship and you can may fall out badly or even decide to finish. If a row ever descends into violence, then it's time to walk away now before you get physically or mentally hurt. Violent personalities rarely change without professional help.

- **Rule breaking**. When you're in any relationship you build up a set of rules; sometimes these aren't even talked about, you just 'know' they're there. The rules are about what you expect from each other (for example, respecting each other's needs, giving each other space sometimes, not repeating secrets). One of the strongest rules is the one about deception – not expecting your friend to cheat on you by dating someone else or telling you lies. If you can't trust the person involved your relationship is almost certainly doomed!

The break up

If the relationship or friendship has been a long one, it can be very difficult to cope well with breaking up. Your lives have been intertwined in many ways and on many levels. So how to you handle it, when it comes to the crunch?

It's probably best to see the break not as an event on its own but as a process that takes time. It's true that 'breaking up is hard to do' because everything that's involved in it makes you feel pretty rotten. There are said to be five stages to a breakdown of a relationship:

- Discovering that you are dissatisfied.

- Telling your partner / friend about it.

- Talking it through.

- Trying to put things right.

- Ending the relationship / friendship.

Nevermind, Shaz. Tell me all about it - I'm all ears!

It's important to remember that you'll probably come out of the relationship giving your other friends an account of its life and death. You'll need to justify its ending, help save face and also keep alive the memories of it. Be kind to yourself, you may need some space and time to get through the grieving period. Try not to do anything in rage and anger you may later regret. The way you cope and get over the break up will prepare you for relationships to come as well as helping you out of old ones.

> 'I cried a lot at first. My parents were very sympathetic and gave me lots of hugs. My best friend was there too to cheer me up. I ripped all the clothes he left at my house and threw his photos out of the window. Then I scribbled all over the letters he's sent me. After a while I calmed down and rang him to shout all sorts of abuse. My final revenge came when I snogged his best mate!'
> (17-YEAR-OLD GIRL)

Staying friends

Many people find it possible to remain friends with the person they are no longer going out with. Sometimes this happens immediately, sometimes it takes time and space to get over the change. The easier you found it to talk to each other in a relationship, the easier it will be to stay friends, because you can both talk through and accept why it's not working anymore. If communication was never very good, and you felt the other person never truly understood you, then maybe you were not really friendship material anyway.

Maintaining other friendships

If you are dating someone, it's never a good idea to spend all your available time with that person, and have none left for your other friends. Good friendships can sometimes be life-long, whilst partnerships can come and go. If you spend all your free time with one person, you risk suffocating them and driving them away. You probably both have different interests you'd like to continue, and not give up because the other person resents your time away from them. It is healthy to have other social activities and independence. If you've ignored friends whilst you've been wrapped up in someone else, and that relationship breaks up, you may find your old friends have moved on, and no longer have time for you in their lives. You will then have to re-build your entire social scene.

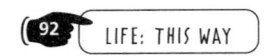

Finishing a relationship

Before even agreeing to see or date someone, ask yourself if you are going out with them for the right reasons, and not because you feel pressured by others or because it will enhance your image. The longer you go out with someone and the more you get involved in each other's lives, the more difficult it can be to end the relationship. Especially if you've reached the point where you know and like the other's family and friends and your whole social life seems to be shared one way or the other. (Remember to try to keep some of your old single way of life if you can, so you have some back up if it doesn't work out.) If you don't feel 100% happy most of the time (make allowances for difficulties which are a normal part of any friendships), then maybe this relationship doesn't really have a long-term future. Don't get stuck in a rut with someone if the relationship is getting boring, argumentative, the other person is trying to control you perhaps by being jealous or possessive. If it's not working for you, and you've tried to make changes to improve things and they are not working, then maybe it's time to move on.

Sometimes your partner may have moved away, and whilst you have vowed to keep up the relationship, the distance and lack of being able to spend time with that person just makes it impossible to try and continue. Neither of you are receiving what you each really want.

How to end it

Usually the other person already has an idea deep down that you are not happy. Your attitude may have changed, you may have become more distant, or rude and nit-picking, and the friendship has started to see lots of changes since it started out. If the person has moved away, you can probably see differences in your letters, e-mails or 'phone conversations – they are no longer as close as they were in the beginning.

> *If that bloke rings again, tell him I never want to see his ugly face again!*
>
> *You tell him yourself!*

If it's time to end the relationship, do it yourself! Don't get someone else to do it, that's cowardly. Don't be cruel either: we all know how much rejection hurts. Telling others before you've told your boyfriend or girlfriend, or going out with someone else or telling lies is unkind. If possible, tell your partner yourself in person. This may not be possible if they've moved away, in which case it may be best to end things in a letter. E-mail is not so personal, and phone calls can be tricky because you can't see each other and communicate as you might like to.

Dear John ...

If you write a letter, keep it as short as possible. You have made the decision it's not going to work, so there is no need to feel bad or guilty. You don't need to justify all your reasons as to why it's not working out. Try if you can to be positive, and not just write a list which could hurt of what you dislike in the other person. You each have the right to be yourselves, even if you are not perfect for each other.

If you see the other person regularly, then pick a time where you can both be alone to tell them of your decision. It's not fair to tell someone at a party where they may not be able to get away without others realising something has upset them. Sometimes this is better in a public place – like a café or park. You may think you may know how the other person is going to react, so if you think they may be so upset that they may react badly indeed (maybe tears or shouting or pleading), then try to choose the time and place carefully to cope with such a situation. If the person is emotional or even violent then you may want to choose somewhere where help is on hand, like at your home, or where friends can be called, or even decide in these circumstances a phone call or letter is best.

Keep it short

Keep the conversation short and to the point. Have a rough idea planned out of what you want to say. The other person may already have an idea and the conversation doesn't prove as difficult as you may have feared. Be firm, don't offer the person any hope of maybe things working out in the future if you know they just won't. Don't be persuaded to change your mind, however much they promise they can improve things between you. If at a later date you both want to give things another go, you both may have that choice.

Trial separations don't usually work either: you'll always be wondering what the other person is up to. If it's over, it's over; don't keep the relationship hanging on by a thread of hope.

How you might feel

Whether a relationship lasted a few days (yet you may have been very excited and hopeful of a positive immediate future), a few weeks, months or even years you may feel some of the following thoughts and stages of grief and disappointment, which could be in varying degrees or order:

- Shock or surprise – *'I had no idea he wanted to finish with me.'*

- Disbelief or denial – *'This is not really happening, it isn't really over.'*

- Guilt – *'If only I'd done this or that, been different.'*

- Anger and frustration – *'She can't do this to me. I'll get my revenge someday.'*

- Depression and apathy – *'What's the point in going out, I'll never find anyone else.'*

- Acceptance – *'Maybe it would have never worked out.'*

- Moving forwards – *'There's no point thinking about what might have been. Time to move onwards and upwards.'*

LIFE: THIS WAY

> 'For me, it begins with anger, then sadness, then denial. You suddenly find yourself depressed and in a pit that you don't think you will get out of. But as time goes on he begins to leave your system. You don't miss him as much and you don't think of him as much and you begin to climb back to human life. Eventually you calm down and experience the bliss of indifference. But it never really goes away completely. You always think about them from time to time.'
>
> (17-YEAR-OLD GIRL)

All the above feelings are really normal, and it's at times like these that you may need to lean on close friends and family for support. Being able to talk your feelings through with someone else can really help your recovery. You may find it helpful to put away everything which reminds you of the other person, like spring-cleaning them out of your life ready for a new beginning. You may not be able to avoid seeing the other person. Just try to act as normal as possible, perhaps in the way you did before you went out together. Being happy is a far better revenge than trying to get your own back on them in someway. Time and comfort from friends is a great healer.

There's plenty more fish in the sea!

BUT YOU DON'T UNDERSTAND 97

LIFE: THIS WAY

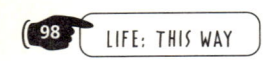

BUT YOU DON'T UNDERSTAND

Chapter 7

THE SAME BUT DIFFERENT

> Yo! You seem different!

> I'm going through a black phase!

> I'd never had guessed!

Individuality

We're all unique individuals and no-one is identical – not even identical twins. There are also ways that you stand out and are different from others, from the way you project yourself to your fashion sense, your image, your abilities, your class / colour / creed and culture. People often say that you shouldn't judge a book by its cover, but first impressions do count. How you look and how you project yourself makes a definite statement about you to others.

> *'I went through my 'black' phase last year. Black everything – nails, eyes, lips, make-up, hair, clothes. I even wanted to paint my room black, but my parents wouldn't have any of it!'*
>
> (15-YEAR-OLD GIRL)

Clothes sense

Clothes can label you as rich or poor, man or woman, English or Indian. Everyone in society is affected by fashion, whether it is trying to keep up with the latest 'look' or making an individual statement. But you don't just wear clothes to be fashionable or to keep warm, it's also an outward sign of you, your character, interests and mood. Whether you like it or not you judge people by what they wear and others judge you in the same way.

Cultures

Many cultures have a distinct way of dressing. That doesn't only mean people from different countries, but also different cultures within a country. They too have their own latest fashion. Could you, for example, pick out a fashionable sari or tell which is the new look for Japan? Some cultures are looking more and more Westernised because these clothes styles are seen as modern and fashionable status symbols.

Trends

There is a lot of media and peer pressure to wear the latest fashion, and you and your family may or may not be able to afford to keep up with these trends. Try to accept there may be limitations on money as to what you can and can't choose to wear until you are out earning for yourself. You may also be asked to conform to family standards of dress code for specific occasions, like a family visit to an elderly relative, a wedding or church event.

Schools and employers usually have codes and rules about dress and appearance. There are usually very good reasons for this, and you will be required to stick to the rules if you want a peaceful life! The reasons may be for identification (army, police, nurses), tradition (weddings, funerals, special events), sports (practicality, identity in cricket or other team games), safety (catering staff, laboratory workers, engineering / agricultural trades), image (bank staff, travel industry staff), and as part of a group (school, youth organisations). Can you think of other areas and other reasons why you may be required to wear certain types of clothing?

You don't understand

When you are away from work or school though, you may be able to express your own individuality in any way you wish. However, some friends and family may not understand why you choose to dress the way you do; others are much more accepting and tolerant and think you are just going through a phase. It may be that your family will allow you to go out dressed as a scruffy mutt with your friends, but ask for a cleaner appearance when attending, say, a family birthday party. Some people will dress differently or have body piercings and tattoos as a way of rebelling, especially if they think they will gain attention as a result and shock their usually conservatively dressed and thinking family. Sometimes this individuality is really only a way of conforming to another group. Many 'New Age' travellers, bikers and other seemingly rebellious groups often end up with their own kind of code of uniform.

Homosexuality

One other way that you might feel different is through your sexuality. A homosexual is a person attracted to the same sex, and this happens in both men and women. A common term used these days is 'gay'. Many people are heterosexual and this means that they are attracted to the opposite sex.

In the recent past homosexuality has not been treated well by most of society and punished with social rejection and the law. Strange, because in ancient Rome, Greece, Egypt and Asian countries it was always considered to be an acceptable practice.

Whatever makes you homosexual, whether it's something you're born with or due to your situation, it's a part of life. Homosexuals are not mad, perverted or immoral, but are people with rights and feelings. Even today, where homosexuals are more accepted than they've ever been, they are still labelled as different and to a certain extent, isolated. Because homosexuals are in the minority in a population, they may want support and understanding from others with the same feelings. There are many support groups which can help people come to terms with feeling different or unhappy, and enable them to grow confident and to meet with others so they don't feel so alone. Many countries are growing more tolerant and relaxing laws which once made homosexuality illegal. Many gay communities and social areas in cities now exist where gay people can socialise and relax without fear of meeting prejudice.

> 'When I found out my mate was gay I was a bit shocked. I thought it was just a rumour, so I asked him. He admitted it, which was a brave thing to do. I don't think I could if I found out I was. I'm too much of a coward.'
> (16-YEAR-OLD BOY)

Family help

Many homosexuals are scared of telling their families. They fear rejection and shame. It's difficult to feel valued and keep your self-respect when even your family don't try to understand. Support is needed from family and friends, but if you can't find it there, then counselling is available to help you through.

In early adolescence it's very common to have a crush on someone of the same sex. Most people outgrow this though, and realise they prefer the opposite sex.

Homosexuality isn't a medical problem; you can't just take a pill and make it go away. It's part of life and the person and why should gays want to change? Being different is just that. It doesn't mean gays are wrong and heterosexuals are right. All it means is that homosexuals are human beings the same as everyone else, except for their sexual preferences.

Other differences

There could be many other differences that might make you feel alone, isolated, and that no-one else could possibly understand you. But you can be certain that there are other people who feel the same way as you or have had similar experiences. There are too many differences to list here, but they could include feeling like you were born in the wrong body (as in you feel you should have been female rather than male), that you were adopted but would like to know who your real parents were, that you have feelings or fears you don't know how to express (such as violence or depression) or phobias (such as a fear of being in public places or of spiders). If you feel unhappy or different about anything and it's seriously limiting or affecting your life, then you probably can't fix the issue alone. Get help. If you haven't a trusted adult or doctor to ask, then check out helplines or organisations that can point you in the right direction. Don't suffer in silence and alone.

Disabilities

Being disabled might be seen as being 'different'. One in ten people in the world has some kind of disability. Often disabled people are seen as just that, and not individuals. They are sometimes judged on what they can't do instead of what they can. In this way some people confuse disability with inability. This can lead to ignorance and lack of respect. It can also mean that disabled people aren't given the same opportunities as the able-bodied.

> *'I wrote to my mate who's in a wheelchair and told her I'd started Line Dancing. She wrote back saying that she was still on wheels, but at least it kept her out of Line Dancing! Cheeky tart!'*
> (17-YEAR-OLD GIRL)

What is a disability?

You can't always tell just by looking if someone is disabled or not. If the brain has been damaged (say at birth or in an accident) then it can't send signals to different parts of the body properly. This means the person may be mentally disabled.

If someone is physically disabled, it means that part of the body has been damaged and isn't able to react to messages sent by the brain. Blindness, deafness and spinal damage are all physical disabilities, as are missing limbs or disfigurations (such as large 'birth marks'). Some people are born disabled, others have been ill or had an accident. Some disabilities can't be cured, others can, and some may become worse as time goes on.

> *'So what! I can't walk. I'm not dead and I've just joined a Circus Skills workshop. Can you juggle five balls at once?'*
> (14-YEAR-OLD GIRL)

Problems to be faced

One of the biggest problems faced by the disabled is other people's attitudes. Some ignore the disabled person and pretend they're not there. Others may be too gushy and try to do too much. Both can be very upsetting if you're the one getting the attention or the ignorance.

> *'So there I was, sitting outside Woolies in my wheelchair waiting for my sister, when this oldish lady came up to me. She smiled, patted me on the head and pressed a 50p into my hand. I was utterly gobsmacked!'*
> (14-YEAR-OLD GIRL)

Work and getting around

This kind of attitude and ignorance from society in general can mean a disabled person finds it difficult to find work. Although there are now equal opportunities laws which say that certain companies must try to employ a number of people with disabilities and provide them with the facilities they require. New buildings must be designed with disabled access and facilities. Many restaurants and other social areas are now also trying to provide easy access and adapted loos which wheelchair users can get to. Other problems include simply getting around. Many older buildings and streets still don't provide enough access for disabled people. Steps, narrow doorways and supermarket aisles can all be a nightmare!

> *'I went to the cinema with my mates only to find there was no way I could get up the steps in my wheelchair. They offered to carry me. No way! We left.'*
> (15-YEAR-OLD BOY)

Check out for yourself how you might negotiate your way around your local area, school, home or work if you were blind, let alone had a problem with walking.

Help at hand?

Some disabled people don't need any help at all, some do and very often don't get all the help they need. They could be because they're:

- scared to ask

- don't like to ask

- don't know what help they can get and/or are entitled to

- don't know how to get the help they're entitled to.

Disabled people can receive help from charities or money for special equipment from the government. The best help is that which doesn't make the person feel different or separated from society. If you want to help a disabled friend, then take the time to find out exactly what the person needs. Ask them what difficulties they have which are extra to those which you face daily. Don't bully them to tell you as it could seem like an intrusion. Just let them know that you are willing to help, and don't mind being asked. There are other groups around to help, too – self-help groups, special classes and organisations providing activities for the disabled and able-bodied.

More severely disabled

The more disabled the person is, the more specialised equipment and treatment is needed. A full-time carer may also be needed, although very often this is a close family member and not uncommonly a child. Being severely disabled can be very difficult for the person, relying on someone else to do things for them. Young carers, too, can feel resentment at having to be there all of the time. They may be missing out on schooling as well as socialising. Respite care is now available in a lot of areas. This is where someone comes in to look after the person to give the carer a break. Counselling could also help, ask your doctor as a first port of call.

Adapting

The way disabled people feel about their disability depends on their individual circumstances. People disabled for a long time may have adapted well to their situation but still find some things hard to accept or adjust to. People who are more recently disabled need time to come to terms with their new life. This may show itself as anger, usually aimed at those closest, and depression. Things have to be relearned, perhaps in a different way. Added to this is the feeling that they don't want to be treated any differently from anyone else.

Many disabled people treat their disability in a 'matter of fact' way and get on with life, trying to make the best of what they have and enjoying it to the full. Some admit that their disability has made them stronger and given them insights into life that they wouldn't otherwise have had. All disabled people want to have the same opportunities as those who are able-bodied.

Disabled people often surprise others in the way that they see their disability as ordinary. They don't picture themselves as brave, they just see themselves as getting on with life and adapting. In this way they have a better understanding of themselves and others.

It's worth remembering all this when you next meet someone who is disabled. See the person and not the disability.

110   LIFE: THIS WAY

Chapter 8
US AND THEM

Prejudice

Are you prejudiced? Do you treat some people differently to others (this is called 'discrimination')? Many of us would like to say 'no', but you may be surprised at how you actually do behave and how many prejudices you have that you perhaps didn't realise were there.

LIFE: THIS WAY

It's a part of human nature; humans like to belong to similar groups. This could be your class at school, drama or boxing club, football or netball team, or the church you go to. It's good to feel you belong.

However, by putting people into groups (even randomly) prejudice and discrimination can be created. We immediately prefer our 'in-group' and will discriminate against the 'out-group'. Even if we don't know the other people in our group, we still favour them over the other group! When you think of the number of groups

Actually, I'm quite a gentle caring sort, who likes flower arranging!

And I didn't fancy sitting next to you!

BUS STOP

Think about it

If you were to get on a half-full bus, and the passengers were a cross-section of your local community (picture all the different people you meet in your area), who would you sit next to, and what would influence your choice?

you belong to, it's not surprising that sometimes tensions can occur. You are not only grouped with your family or friends, but in bigger groups according to your skin colour, age, gender, level of fitness, and where you live.

> *'Now I come to think about it, I belong to quite a few different groups. My tutor group at school, my school, my sports club, my family, my friendship group – I could go on and on!'*
> (13-YEAR-OLD GIRL)

What is prejudice and discrimination?

When you dislike or favour a person or group based on a pre-formed belief and stereotype, it's called prejudice. Although this may be wrong, it's something we all do unfortunately, and in itself it isn't a crime.

If you treat people unfairly because of your prejudice, then this behaviour is called discrimination. Many forms of discrimination are against the law; for example, sexism – perhaps a person doesn't get offered a job because of their sex, and isn't judged solely on their suitability. Racism (pre-judging people by the race they belong to) is a prejudice which can create such strong feelings that it can lead to violent behaviour against other people. Sexism, ageism and all other forms of discrimination in our society need to be questioned. We all have the right to be treated equally and the right to live in safety.

LIFE: THIS WAY

Getting rid of prejudice

You'd have thought we'd have stamped out prejudice, especially after passing laws against sex and race discrimination. But prejudice still exists, for example, not employing a 44-year-old because they're too old, or the belief that an older person is stupid just because they don't understand the finer points of a 'Tomb Raider II' computer game.

Just because I'm a dog, doesn't mean I'm dim!

Another form of discrimination is based on the way people (usually women) look. Some women feel they have a hard time if they have good looks and a brain! No-one expects a pretty girl to be a brainy one! If people are overweight, they are thought of by some as unattractive, unfashionable but very jolly. Of course this is total rubbish, but alas it happens.

> 'When we went skiing we had to share the coach with another school. They all looked a bit weird when they got on. As the week passed though, we got to know them and they were a really good laugh. I'm even writing to one girl.'
> (15-YEAR-OLD BOY)

So in spite of all sorts of laws against discrimination, community and media education, and television and radio programmes for minority groups, the problem is still a big one. Prejudice will never be eliminated as some groups of people will always consider themselves better than others, whether it's the team choice of a group of football supporters or members of an expensive or exclusive club.

Changing attitudes

Unfortunately once we are prejudiced we tend to ignore any information which might change the first attitude or belief we formed. Even in its mild form, prejudice can lead to hurtful behaviour towards people. In its worst form it can lead to murder and genocide (the murder of a whole group or race of people, for example, ethnic cleansing as in the Holocaust).

> *'I don't like people whose eyes are too close together, those who have wobbly chins, loose lips, people who slurp their tea, or sneeze like a cat, although they are probably very nice.'*
> (14-YEAR-OLD GIRL)

Stereotyping, or putting people into slots because we don't know enough about them as individuals, is where prejudice starts. Those who are racially prejudiced tend to see all black people or all Germans or Chinese as being the same. They fail to see that the race is in fact made up of individuals, some who are good, some bad, some violent, some not – but all individuals. Another example is the way that other countries view each other. They base their attitude on the behaviour of a few football supporters, or a stereotypical view ('all French people eat frog's legs', 'all Japanese carry cameras', 'the Dutch have no sense of humour', 'all British football supporters cause trouble'), then believe that all the peoples must be the same!

LIFE: THIS WAY

Think about it

Xenophobia means a dislike of foreigners. What preconceived ideas do you have about other countries? Where did these ideas come from? Do you know? Now who do you actually know from one of these countries, and how do they compare to the stereotypical view?

Understanding where prejudice comes from

So why does it happen? There have been many reasons suggested and put forward:

- Some societies are more racist or prejudiced than others. People in these societies will tend to go along with the majority. For example, the United Kingdom is far more tolerant of different groups than, say, Arab countries or the USA. Peaceful demonstrations and marches, speaker's corners (places where anyone can get up on a box and speak on almost anything) are accepted ways of life, but these and other activities would be banned or not tolerated in other countries.

- 'Scapegoating' is another reason. This is when people are fed up or frustrated and they take it out on others. If we feel threatened, we need someone to blame. Scapegoats are usually minority groups in society (Jews, travellers, gypsies, blacks, gays ...).

- Some people have very rigid narrow-minded personalities, and it's been found that these people are more likely to be prejudiced than others. They are usually prejudiced against any group not like their own.

- Research has suggested that prejudice also develops from the way you are brought up. Parents may pass on their views and attitudes to their children. Children may also learn prejudices from other people they look up to and admire.

- When people are randomly put into any kind of group, it causes prejudice, especially if they're competing for the same thing – land, food or even sports competitions.

Reducing prejudice

The bad news is prejudice is harder to change than any other kind of attitude. Harder, but not impossible.

The Eye of the Storm

A few years ago, a teacher of 9-year-olds in the USA wanted to give the children the opportunity to experience the evils of prejudice and discrimination, in a safe setting (the classroom). She told her class one day that brown-eyed people were more intelligent and 'better' than those with blue eyes. She explained that the brown eyes would rule the class and they were given extra privileges over blue-eyed children, who were to be 'kept in their place'. Blue-eyed children were last in line, seated at the back of the classroom and had to wear special collars to show their 'low status'.

After a short time the blue-eyed children's schoolwork began to suffer, they were depressed, angry and described themselves negatively. Brown-eyed children became mean, made the most of their power and made nasty comments to the blue-eyed children.

The next day the teacher announced that she'd lied and it was really blue-eyed children who were better. The pattern of prejudice and discrimination switched very quickly. The teacher ended the study and talked to the class about what had happened and how they felt. All of them agreed that being thought to be of a lower status, wasn't a nice feeling.

It would be good to think that the benefits of taking part in this study lasted, but we don't know whether they did or not.

Tackling prejudice

Research has shown that prejudice can be reduced if a situation is set up where people are seen as individuals and not just part of their stereotyped group. It is thought that five conditions need to be met if prejudice is to be tackled and reduced:

1. Equal Status. People from different groups should be on the same equal level and one shouldn't be viewed to be of a lower or higher status than the other.

2. Personal Contact. People from different groups need to meet and get to know each other as individuals. Have more contact with people who don't fit into the stereotypes held, so real personalities are seen.

3. Support from society (or someone in some kind of authority). Some education and social support is needed – from teachers, the media, the government, or the police, for example – for attitudes to change and to make sure minority groups are treated fairly.

4. Working Together. Doing something together and working towards a common goal is one of the biggest prejudice reducers.

LIFE: THIS WAY

> ### Think about it
>
> **Can you think of any ideas which would help reduce prejudice and discrimination for the five points above? For example combined church services, inter-school or group team sports, working on a community project such as a youth club or play area, disabled and able-bodied events such as a drama club.**

If all five points are met prejudice can be reduced – but all five are needed. If one of the areas is missing then the contact can break down. So all is not lost. As a society we are trying to address the problems of all kinds of prejudice that people hold. Changes won't be made overnight, though. It will take time and a lot of understanding. Can you help by being more tolerant or accepting of others?

BUT YOU DON'T UNDERSTAND 121

122 LIFE: THIS WAY

BUT YOU DON'T UNDERSTAND

Chapter 9

IT'S A GOAL!

Needs and wants

It can be difficult to realise that all of us have needs. We all need to be understood, we need food and shelter, friends and respect from others and we need to feel safe. We also need to understand others, but before we can do that properly, we need to make sense of ourselves. Perhaps one of the highest needs of all is to achieve a full understanding of ourselves so that we can be the best that we possibly can.

LIFE: THIS WAY

The needs that we have through our lives can be put in order. Once the first set of needs are satisfied then the next set becomes most important to us, then the next and so on. But at any time the first set of needs must be satisfied.

Need for:

1. food, water, oxygen, shelter, water, rest

2. safety, security, protection from illness

3. friends, acceptance by others, trust, loving, being loved

4. self-confidence, respect from others

5. meaning, knowledge and experience of life

6. beauty, balance

7. becoming everything you're capable of being, total fulfilment.

The Level 1 needs must be met first, otherwise you wouldn't survive. Once that's met you can move on to level two, then three and so on.

Think about it

Where do you think you are on the scale? What else do you need? What else do you want to achieve?

> *'My dreams for the future are still to be alive (obviously). To do some kind of work in Biological Science. I'm also looking forward to seeing how powerful computers will become and how they will change our life. I'm also worried we're going to destroy ourselves.'*
>
> (17-YEAR-OLD BOY)

Destiny

Trying to satisfy your needs in this way can be a driving force. The important issue here is that we can be in control of much of our own destiny. You can make things happen, good or bad, by how you behave, your attitudes to others and by the situations you find yourself in. It's difficult sometimes to keep 'control' of our own lives and yet this is probably where the key to success lies.

Sometimes life throws you a curved ball that takes you completely unawares. Major life changes like parents separating, unemployment, lack of money, redundancy, bereavement are some of the things that can happen that you have absolutely no control over. There's no doubt that these can affect the goals that you have set for yourself in life.

Check out the DON'T GIVE ME GRIEF book in the series for more about life changes

> *'I want to find something I'm really good at, which I can be proud of myself for doing. Mainly I want to be happy and content with whatever career I choose. At the moment I have difficulty seeing anything I am particularly talented at.'*
>
> (17-YEAR-OLD GIRL)

Control and change

Sometimes you have to forget one plan or ambition, and try to make your way in another completely different direction. You have to learn to adjust and cope with these changes and to put them down to experiences that help you to grow.

Another factor to look at is whether the change is under your control or not. The amount of control you feel you have will make a great difference to how you cope. Children in Samoa, for example take on adult-type roles from about five years of age. They copy and help with adult jobs and as children grow they take on more and more of the adult work. They don't find adolescence to be such a sudden major change, and so don't find it as stressful as we do in our society. The change from being a child into an adult is under their control and is very gradual.

Dreams for the future

We all need dreams and ambitions, and goals and targets to set to help us achieve them. What are your goals for the next three years? What about the next ten years?

> 'My main dream is to win the lottery – same as every other person. But if not, then I want to be successful in whatever career I choose.'
>
> (16-YEAR-OLD GIRL)

Take a few moments to jot down your dreams and goals for the future. Are your plans and hopes achievable? Are they realistic? For example, wanting to be a pilot would need focused study and qualifications. Going to university would mean passing A-level exams. Owning your own car would mean saving and money management. How might your expectations and goals be realised? It's surprising when you look back, to see if you're where you wanted to be, or if you've changed direction completely and are blissfully happy doing something else!

> 'Dreams for the future for me are a large expensive house, a fast car and a financially secure and exciting job with a family. My general dream would include world peace!'
>
> (17-YEAR-OLD BOY)

Some goals that people set for themselves may include:

By 14 years: I want my gold swimming badge.
(This could be achieved by setting a training schedule and sticking to it, working on improving swimming techniques.)

By 16 years: I want a good set of GCSE results.
(This could be achieved by working out a study and revision plan. Doing your best in class. Asking for help, or extra teaching support.)

By 18 years I want to be travelling.
(This could be achieved by saving money for a rail travel pass and camping and working around Europe. It could also be achieved in many other ways such as being an au pair, doing voluntary work overseas, taking part in a sponsored youth adventure team trip.)

By 19 years: I want to have passed my driving test. Good A-levels, or an interesting job.
(First start saving for the driving lessons, see if there's a part-time

weekend job you can get, and set a savings plan. If you have an idea of the career you might want to try for, choose A levels that will be appropriate for that job.)

> *'In the future I want to get good A level results, go to uni, have a fantastic time, get a good job and meet a nice bloke!'*
> (17-YEAR-OLD GIRL)

The bottom line is that you are the only one to have first-hand experience of yourself as a person. You know what you are and deep down you also know what you're capable of and what you could be. You have the ability to move your life forward. Sometimes problems will crop up or there will be things that cause you pain or that you're not too satisfied with. These will need to be dealt with and seen as part of life's experiences.

What I am and what I can do

Although you may not realise it, you judge every experience you have in terms of yourself. Most of us try to keep a balance between the way other people see us and how we behave. Sometimes, though this doesn't happen. For example you may see a friend as very clever, but he may think of himself as stupid and a failure. If this happens and there's a big gap between how others see you and how you see yourself then it can stop you from growing and changing as a person and the less likely you are to reach your goals in life.

Self-worth

From when you were little, you learn to act and feel in ways that earn you approval from others, rather than the way you really would like to act. You may push away feelings and behaviour that wouldn't make other people happy. This is so that you feel liked by others and have 'worth'. The problem here is that you may actually behave, think and feel in certain ways just because others want you to and this could lead to problems. Some people go through their whole lives trying to live by other people's standards instead of their own. Be true to yourself.

Family help

If you live in an atmosphere where your parents and family offer support and acceptance then you're more likely to accept certain thoughts and feelings as your own instead of trying to disown them. Friends and family who care about you will accept you even when you make mistakes. Though they may be angry and not like your behaviour a whole lot at the time, they love you enough to forgive you. This kind of atmosphere allows you to grow in leaps and bounds! It's an atmosphere where there's understanding.

132 LIFE: THIS WAY

BUT YOU DON'T UNDERSTAND

Chapter 10
SLUGS AND SPICE

> Sugar and spice and all things nice, that's what little girls are made of.
> Slugs and snails and puppy dogs' tails, that's what little boys are made of!

Do what?

Boys and girls, women and men, male and female

The writer George Orwell wrote 'All animals are equal but some animals are more equal than others' in his book, *Animal Farm*. Every human should be seen and treated as equal, but of course every person is also different and has different opportunities and levels of ability in all areas. Male and female human beings are different too.

Different bodies, different reproductive systems, different muscle tone, different brain sizes – and certainly different thought processes and priorities. No matter how equal the opportunities and upbringing even girl and boy twins will behave and react in different ways. Most boys tend to be more socially physical and aggressive, most girls seem to think and discuss aspects of their life more. What you can't expect is for any person to think or behave in exactly the way you do, especially if they are the opposite sex to you.

> **Think about it**
>
> Now that you are older, have you ever closely watched toddlers playing? Have you seen five-year-olds at play in the school playground? What are the differences even at this early age? Are the boys rushing about, tumbling and tackling? Are the girls playing more gentle games, or talking in groups? What are their reactions if there is a problem do the boys get physically aggressive? Do the girls cry?

Definitely different

You have seen the different ways men and boys, girls and women behave and socialise at school, at home and at work. You have seen crowd activities and crime first-hand or on the news. You may have noticed the different kinds of sports, social activities and hobbies most males or females tend to enjoy. And who likes to watch what kinds of film or television programme in your home? What do you think about the differences you have experienced? Just as we may pre-judge people from other countries and cultures, males and females make different judgements about each other – for example, women are romantic and men never remember special occasions like an anniversary. For our final chapter, the last words go to some young people aged between 11 and 16 years, who may or may not have an understanding of the opposite sex!

Girls talking about boys

Some boys are very childish and ignore you. I like to see them dressed up when they go somewhere posh.

Boys get a buzz out of using you then dumping you. They always have to be in charge, that's their leading role.

Lads are sometimes sarcastic about some of the most simple things and take it too far which upsets girls. I'd like someday to find a partner who is a good laugh and sometimes romantic.

They think they are big and bad. They use you and like to have your money off you.

If they get too close to you, they become really possessive.

Boys always think they are the best at everything.

Lads can get away with much more than girls. It's all right if a lad swears, they get away with it, but for a girl it's unladylike.

They flirt all the time with other girls. But I like it when they make nice comments about you.

I like the feel of a boy's arms around me. It makes me feel really safe.

I don't like it when they show off and have a bad attitude. Some of them cry when they get detention.

I read somewhere that 70% of men forget Valentine's Day.

Boys think they are tough and cool. I do like boys when they are kind and caring towards a girl.

Some of them have a sad personality and can never keep secrets, they don't know how to impress a girl.

Boys talking about girls

Most girls have no feelings for people. Most boys like good looks and a good personality in girls.

They are extremely bossy and can get on your nerves. They are very annoying because they always cry for little reasons. If you ask them if they want some food they always say 'No', then nick your food afterwards. Some of them have a good personality though.

Aaahhh, cute dog!

100% correct!

Girls always spend hours doing their hair and make-up. They can never decide what clothes to wear. They have to have everything perfect.

Some girls are not very honest. Like when they do not turn up where they say they are going to meet you.

They spend a lot of money and sometimes ignore you.

Girls think they know everything, have a bad attitude and mood swings.

BUT YOU DON'T UNDERSTAND

They annoy me when an animal comes on TV and they go 'Aahhhh'.

Girls never get told off at school. They answer more questions so boys don't have to put their hands up.

Girls are nice and soft. It's their skin I think – so soft.

I don't like girls because they worry too much about their hair and are sarcastic.

The thing I hate about girls is their short temper. My mum is no exception. Some girls do like sport and I like that.

Girls are forever talking. They moan at you, then want to walk with you. Some are OK.

Girls are two-timers who only want you for your money.

I like to hear girls talk, it's so different to us lads when we talk.

LIFE: THIS WAY

Appendix

Useful Contacts (UK)

Some basic info

Your school, local library, Citizens' Advice Bureau, borough or county council, social services, health or community centre, the Internet and local telephone directories will all have contact numbers, emergency helplines, addresses and details for every kind of organisation, help or charity you may need.

Helplines are manned by trained counsellors, some of whom are volunteers. Whatever you want to ask or say, they will know how to help you, and many of the issues or questions raised have been heard many times before.

Many helplines have free phone numbers and offer support, counselling and referral to other organisations. Some numbers will not even appear on a telephone bill. This means you could make a call, and no-one will know. Ask the helpline when you call.

Some helplines are very busy, and some are open at restricted times only. Don't give up, keep trying and you will get through. Have a pen and paper in case an answerphone message gives you information you need to note down, or if you are referred to another group or organisation to contact. You do not need to give your name and address to confidential helplines if you don't want to, the person answering will just refer to you as 'Caller'. Calls are treated in strictest confidence.

Here are just a few of the lines and organisations available:

- **Childline** – a helpline for all kinds of problems children may experience, including abuse and being at risk:
  ☎ **0800 1111**

- **LIFE** – for counselling and help with all kinds of issues surrounding pregnancy and abortion
  ☎ **01962 311511** and **020 7825 2500** (9am to 5pm)

- **Crimestoppers**
  ☎ **0800 555 111**

- **National Drugsline**
  ☎ **0800 776 600**

- **Quitline**
  ☎ **0800 002 200**

- **Drinkline**
  ☎ **0345 320 202**

- **Equal Opportunities Commission**
  ☎ **0161 833 9244**

- **Disability Discrimination** – freepost Bristol BS38 7DG

- **Raleigh International**
  ☎ **0207 371 8585**

- **Voluntary Service Overseas**
  ☎ **020 8780 7500** 🌐 **www.vso.org.uk**

LIFE: THIS WAY

- **Samaritans** help for those in despair or feeling suicidal:
  ☎ **0345 909090** *if you can't remember this number and need it in an emergency, just dial* **100** *and ask the operator to put you through to the Samaritans.*
  🌐 **www.samaritans.org.uk**

- **Sexwise** a helpline for teenagers with questions and issues surrounding sex, contraception and sexuality:
  ☎ **0800 282930** *this number will not appear on a bill payers' telephone bill.*

- **Saneline** for support, advice and information to do with all kinds of mental health problems, whether for yourself, or another person you are close to. Hours 12 noon–2pm:
  ☎ **0345 678000**

- **Friend** for people unsure about their sexuality or wanting to talk about their feelings of homosexuality, lesbianism or bisexuality. Offers advice and counselling. Also available for parents. Local counselling groups too. ☎ **020 7837 3337** 7.30pm–10pm everday

- **Terence Higgins Trust** for information and advice about HIV and AIDS. Lines open 24 hours: ☎ **0800 567123 (National Aids Helpline)** also helpline 12 noon–10pm daily on: ☎ **020 7242 1010** 🌐 **www.tht.org.uk**

- **Disability Sport England**
  ☎ **0207 490 4919**

- **National Association of Volunteer Bureaux**
  ☎ **0121 633 4555**
  NAVB database of voluntary opportunities:
  🌐 **www.thesite.org**